OBESITY

Daniel E. Harmon

ROSEN PUBLISHING®

New York

Published in 2007 by The Rosen Publishing Group, Inc.
29 East 21st Street, New York, NY 10010

Library of Congress Cataloging-in-Publication Data

Harmon, Daniel E.
Obesity / Daniel E. Harmon.—1st ed.
    p. cm.—(Coping in a changing world)
Includes bibliographical references and index.
ISBN-13: 978-1-4042-0949-7
ISBN-10: 1-4042-0949-2 (lib. bdg.)
1. Obesity—Juvenile literature. I. Title. II. Series.
RC628.H37 2007
616.3'98—dc22

                                              2006019055

Printed in China

Contents

CHAPTER ONE

A National Epidemic

FOR YOUNG PEOPLE IN THE TWENTY-FIRST CENTURY, IT'S DIFFICULT NOT TO GET CAUGHT UP IN A FAT-BOUND DAILY ROUTINE.

H uman weight is a big problem in
America—in more ways than one. It
affects not just individuals but society
as a whole. It's easier, now more than ever, to
become fat. Obesity, the condition of having an
excessive amount of body fat, is such a serious
concern that health professionals have begun to
attach the "E" word to it: epidemic.

Americans don't need to look hard to understand why. Schools, sidewalks, shopping malls,
and supermarkets are increasingly populated by
large, slow-moving people. If you're at a healthy,
comfortable weight yourself, perhaps you frown
in disgust at the sight. Perhaps you poke fun—but
you'd better not do it too loudly, because you
might not realize (yet) how easy it is to pile on
some pounds.

And if you're already in the "overweight" or "at
risk" zones of the national Centers for Disease
Control and Prevention's body mass index (BMI)
chart, you probably know how it feels. You know
how it feels to huff and puff to keep up with your
classmates, and to be the last person selected
when they choose sides for a pickup basketball or
baseball game. You know how it feels to be called
"wide load." You know how it feels when popular
students avoid you, fearing association with you
will damage their reputations. You might chuckle
at their teasing, but you aren't laughing inside.

If you're among the overweight (being too
heavy for your height), you have lots of company.
One in three young Americans between the ages of

six and nineteen has a significant weight problem. As of 2002, 16 percent of young people in that age range were already considered overweight; another 15 were considered "at risk" of becoming so.[1] Three times as many children are overweight now than were overweight thirty years ago.[2] One recent study that traced the stature of thousands of children reported that by the time they were nineteen, almost half of the white girls and more than half of the African American girls were heavier than they should be.[3] In *Livin' Large: African American Sisters Confront Obesity*, authors Stacy Ann Mitchell and Teri D. Mitchell define obesity as "a chronic disease that can be fatal."[4]

The body mass index chart (discussed in chapter 5) is formulated to help you determine whether you are at a healthy, unhealthy, or at-risk weight. Generally, a BMI rating of 25 to 30 is considered overweight; people with a BMI score of 30 or above are considered excessively overweight, or obese. Note, however, that BMI interpretations vary slightly for those under age twenty because the body's natural fat ratios change with the growth process; normal fat percentages also differ between boys and girls.

Health officials are concerned about weight problems in all age groups, but especially among teenagers. Frances M. Berg, in her book *Underage & Overweight*, explains, "The sobering statistics for overweight teenagers are of particular concern because the older they are, the more likely it is they will become overweight adults."[5]

Medical professionals also are alarmed at evidence of increasing weight problems among preschool children. More than 20 percent of American children from the ages of three to five are either overweight or at risk of becoming so.[6] By spring 2006, automakers were having to design larger safety seats to accommodate overweight preschoolers. Almost 300,000 American children from one to six years old, research indicates, face car safety risks when squeezed into regular safety seats.[7]

A PROBLEM OF ALL AGE GROUPS

This is not merely a children's problem, of course. Research suggests that most Americans today weigh too much. Sixty-five percent of adults are overweight or obese, according to the National Center for Health Statistics.[8] The percentage is rising. As recently as the mid-1990s, "only" 55.9 percent of Americans were overweight. Unless the country's obesity epidemic is contained, obesity is expected to surpass smoking as the leading cause of preventable death.[9] Dr. Sylvia Rimm, in *Rescuing the Emotional Lives of Overweight Children*, writes, "No other disease or health condition even comes close to being so widespread across America."[10]

But why are health care professionals so concerned? Apart from the unhappiness individuals feel about their appearance, is there really anything wrong with being fat?

This book will examine some of the very real and very dangerous risks of obesity. Among young people, one major concern is the connection between excessive fat and the spread of type 2 diabetes. Another is the increasing rate of heart-related ailments. Obesity, studies have shown repeatedly, contributes to a variety of physical problems. If Americans can reverse the nation's bulging trend, those problems can in many cases be prevented.[11]

IS "BAD FOOD" TO BLAME?

No single culprit has brought about America's weight crisis. Accusing fingers point in many directions. One frequent target of critics is the food industry—particularly fast-food chain restaurants and sellers of "junk food" groceries. It's true that food vendors have made calorie-laden foods inexpensive and convenient to prepare and consume. It's also true that they spend billions of dollars on tantalizing ad campaigns to persuade us to buy. If you're like the average American child, it's estimated that you see more than 38,000 television commercials each year. Many of them, as you know, tout not-so-healthy food products.[12]

Some Americans are going to court, suing food companies for their personal weight problems. Others reason that to accuse a food producer of making you fat is a little like accusing a car manufacturer of selling you a car with which you cause an accident while speeding. Automakers, like food companies, spend billions of dollars advertising their products—and most cars can attain unsafe speeds. You choose whether to drive your car sensibly or recklessly. Likewise, all kinds of foods are readily available; you choose to eat sensibly or recklessly.

As a forty-one-year-old New Hampshire woman who's battled obesity since childhood acknowledged to a journalist, "The reality is it's each person's responsibility. You put the food on your plate. You choose whether to eat it."[13] James Tillotson, a professor at Tufts University's Friedman School of Nutrition, observes, "We want to blame somebody, but the thing is, we're all a part of it."[14]

IS EXERCISE A THING OF THE PAST?

For young people in the twenty-first century, it's difficult *not* to get caught up in a fat-bound daily routine. Not only are Americans more accustomed than ever to eating (and eating unhealthy foods), they're less accustomed than ever to moving their bodies. The modern inventor seems bent on making life as easy as possible. People have automated every physical chore from opening cans and brushing their teeth to getting about from place to place and entertaining themselves.

Consider the typical school day of American children fifty or sixty years ago. The morning began for most youngsters with a hearty breakfast. Two out of three either walked or rode bikes to school.[15] Cafeteria lunches may not have been especially tasty, but they usually were prepared according to the accepted standards of a balanced diet. Students enjoyed a recess period during which they organized quick ballgames, skipped rope, ran about the school grounds (supervised, of course), and let off steam. In many schools, they were required to take a physical education (PE) or gym class several times each week, if not daily. After school, they bounded outside to play. In the evening they enjoyed a home-cooked, balanced meal. Homework time followed. Parents might have allowed an hour or two of television viewing—assuming the family had a TV set.

Does your day follow that routine? More likely, your breakfast consists of sugared cereal. You're transported to school by car or bus. (Just one in ten students now walk or pedal.[16]) You take a prepackaged lunch of processed food—or cash with which to buy pizza or burgers, as well as snacks. There may be a free school period, but it probably doesn't resemble the old-fashioned recess. Only a third of American public school-children by the turn of the twenty-first century were taking daily PE classes.[17] Arriving home in the afternoon, you grab a processed "instant meal" or snack from the pantry or freezer. Your choices are tempting indeed: microwavable pizza, maca-roni with cheese, tater tots, buttered breadsticks, corn dogs, "pockets," a box of mini-cheeseburgers, lasagna, meatloaf with gravy, and barbecued chicken wings. You take this into your bedroom or living room to eat. There, you spend an hour or two unwinding with video games or television while munching. Dinner—often take-out fast food—comes a few hours later. If you're not too sleepy after you complete your homework, you finish your day with more television or Internet browsing and e-mail exchanges.

You had plenty to eat, but how much exercise did you get during the day?

A WEIGHT-GAIN "CONSPIRACY"

Decreasing exercise and incorrect nutrition are unquestionably the two leading causes of excess weight. But many other factors, some of them quite subtle, contribute to the problem.

For example, most people are encouraged to eat larger portions of food—especially food that's high in calories. Large and extra-large bottles of soft drinks cost little more than regular sizes, so consumers think they're getting a bargain. Likewise, bonus packages of chips and other snacks give consumers perhaps 30 to 50 percent more to eat for only a few extra pennies. Restaurants offer variations of burgers that consist of so much meat and so many layers of ingredients that diners can't stretch their lips over them. To ensure that their children are never hungry, parents serve more food at mealtime than the whole family possibly can devour. The more they serve, the more everybody is likely to dish out and eat, regardless of how hungry they really are. Studies have indicated that people eat as much as 30 percent more food from larger servings than smaller (but still ample) servings.[18]

Some are eating more in response to stress. And there's the popularity factor: if your popular classmates regularly consume unhealthy foods and sodas for lunch and snacks, don't you feel tempted to join them?

Many children who are overweight live in denial. They see no easy way to change their physical condition, so they pretend it's natural. Parents often reinforce this excuse. "It runs in our family," they frequently explain. It may or may not run in the family. Regardless, it's a challenge that can be taken on effectively.

Sharron Dalton, a professor at New York University's Department of Nutrition, Food Studies, and Public Health, asserts that obesity "is arguably the most pervasive and serious threat to children's health today and in the future." In her book *Our Overweight Children: What Parents, Schools, and Communities Can Do to Control the Fatness Epidemic*, Dalton observes that the childhood obesity epidemic "shows no sign of abating. . . . The accelerating rate indicates that the current generation of children will grow into the most obese generation of adults in history."[19]

DON'T DESPAIR

Despite the gloomy reports Americans hear constantly about their overweight children and teenagers, they can be optimistic. If you are overweight, or if you're concerned about a friend or relative who is, be assured that the problem is solvable. Al Roker, a popular television news personality seen on NBC's *Today* show and other programs, confides, "As an overweight teen, I endured taunts, self-doubt, ridicule, and disdain from all parties in my life, family and friends included. Some of it was intentional, some of it not."[20] Dr. Fred Pescatore, an author and media commentator on weight issues, says that as a child he was so fat he dreaded having to take off his shirt in gym class. "I longed to be just like the rest of the kids, able to look into a mirror without flinching."[21] Roker and Pescatore are among countless examples of overweight people who confronted and overcame their physical quandary and the unhappiness it caused. You can, too.

CHAPTER TWO

Plump Societies, Yesteryear and Now

AS RECENTLY AS THE MID-1900S, SOME OF THE WOMEN WHO WERE CONSIDERED GLAMOROUS AND SHAPELY WOULD BE REGARDED AS A BIT HEAVY TODAY.

A re you worried about your weight? It may interest you to know that countless "heavy" people over the centuries weren't at all worried about theirs. In fact, they were proud of it. At certain times and places in history, men and women actually have wanted to be plump—and even downright fat. For many, it was a status symbol, proof that the person was well-to-do. Stoutness has also been considered stylish by fashion trendsetters of certain generations. Remarkably, it has even been thought to indicate good health.

Make no mistake: Obesity today is a national health crisis. Especially troubling are the rising percentages of overweight young people. To view the issue in full perspective, though, it's best to consider what your ancestors looked like, what they *wanted* to look like, and why.

WHEN POUNDS WERE POSITIVES

A century ago, two doctors wrote a book titled *Vitalogy or Encyclopedia of Health and Home*. In it, they provided instructions to make readers "fleshy or plump."[1] In those years, this was a desirable trait of adults and especially of children. Healthy babies were fat babies. Healthy children were rosy, round-cheeked, fleshy children. Many mothers, concerned about youngsters who looked a bit puny, served liberal portions of hot, hearty (and rather fattening) foods prepared specifically to "stick to your ribs." To be skinny was more to

be avoided than to be fat. A slender figure was
considered unhealthy.

How could that be? In a nutshell, it was because
those days were markedly different from today.
For many of our ancestors, life was difficult. Great
numbers of nineteenth-century immigrants came
to the United States largely because of hard times
in their homelands. Even here, in more stable
communities, countless early American families
depended directly on farming (and therefore on
the weather and other unpredictable factors) for
their livelihoods. It was a challenge for them to
put food on the table day by day, year by year.
Parents did not want their children to be—or to
look—malnourished. Plumpness suggested you
enjoyed a degree of independence and prestige
most people lacked.

Physical strength was a highly valued charac-
teristic, too. While parents wanted their children
to "flesh out," they also wanted them to be
tough—able to take on the world. Exercise back
then was important, but it wasn't a great social
issue because most people got ample exercise in
their ordinary routines. They didn't own the time-
saving, energy-saving conveniences people have
today. In order to get things done, they *had* to
exercise.

CHANGING NOTIONS OF BEAUTY

In photographs from the 1800s and in paintings
from centuries before, you may notice the body

sizes of many of the people depicted. Women, in particular, were frequently plump by today's standards of attractiveness. Many had fat stomachs, fat breasts, and fat bottoms—and they were among the beauty queens of their time. As recently as the mid-1900s, some of the women who were considered glamorous and shapely would be regarded as a bit heavy today. Many believe that Marilyn Monroe, one of the most famous Hollywood icons of the twentieth century, wore size 16 dresses.[2] (There is some dispute about whether Monroe wore size 16 dresses. Dress sizes have changed over the years. A size 16 today is not the same as a size 16 in the 1950s and 1960s.)

Our ideas of what's beautiful and what isn't change from time to time. During the 1920s, fashion-conscious women wanted to have flat chests. During the 1930s, they became intrigued with the buxom, curvy bodies of popular movie actresses. The new attitude may have resulted from the Great Depression, which began soon after the 1929 stock market crash and spread appalling poverty worldwide. Food and fleshy bodies were not so common. Therefore, they became highly desirable.[3]

The interest in well-developed body sizes among women continued after the Depression and World War II (1939–1945). By then, the public was captivated by films and the new medium of television. The best-known actresses were the shapely ones. Many teenage girls yearned to look like them.

Today, the ideal female body is still shapely, but it is slimmer than the ideal of fifty years ago. Women and adolescent girls strive to tone themselves and distribute their weight in "the right places." So do males. Men and boys seem less concerned with their physical shape than females, studies show, but they generally see muscle tone as the key benchmark of attractiveness. Fat tissue, in the minds of most males and females alike, is undesirable.

A "GROWING" PROBLEM FOR YOUNG PEOPLE

While Hollywood was telling twentieth-century Americans how they should look, lifestyles began to change. These changes made it more and more difficult to develop and maintain a Hollywood body. Shifts in food production and marketing, exercise patterns, and more subtle aspects of American life gave rise to the weight woes many Americans face today.

A century ago, "obesity" was a term doctors occasionally used in describing overweight patients who were unable to lose weight even when they tried. Most doctors assumed the problem stemmed from an abnormal thyroid gland or other condition that caused the person's body to store fat. In fact, doctors today know that in certain cases, glandular abnormalities can lead to obesity. But that is not the common cause. In most cases, obesity results from an energy imbalance. That is, obese people consume more energy—calories—than they burn up in physical exercise.[4]

The obesity problem among young people is a relatively recent phenomenon. The trend in higher weight began in the 1960s. Sixteen percent of adolescent Americans are overweight. This may not seem alarming, but during the 1960s, only 5 percent of children were considered overweight.[5] (And remember that now, another 15 percent weigh in as being "at risk.")

Only in the past few years has the term "epidemic" been used to define the situation. Medical professionals observe that some parents realize their children are overweight but refuse to address the problem. Some don't see it as a problem at all; they—like their ancestors—consider extra-large size to be a symbol of health and status. Others sense there is peril ahead, but assume (or hope) that the youth will simply "grow out of it."[6] For many years, some parents have actually contributed to their children's weight problems. If a child is frail, for example, the parents may offer sweets and other tasty but unhealthy types of food in hopes of getting the youngster to eat more. In a few cases, these measures work. In others, they work all too well: The child develops gluttonous eating habits and gradually becomes obese.

In some families, parents frown on their children's weight but provide little useful guidance in controlling it. Research has suggested that 40 percent of nine- and ten-year-old girls (including those of average weight) are weight conscious. Why? Most notably, those surveyed indicated they feel pressure from their mothers to control their weight.[7]

"I Wanna Be a Star"

Mari, thirteen years old, was excited when her middle school announced a new drama club. She nurtured a serious interest in act-ing. Mari harbored no illusions of becoming the next teen idol. She knew in her heart that she had theatrical talent, though. Her par-ents and several friends sensed it, too, and encouraged her. She was eager to see what she could do onstage.

But Mari had a problem. Standing barely 5 feet (1.5 meters) tall, she weighed 140 pounds (64 kilograms). Studying her profile in her bedroom mirror, Mari was overwhelmed by despair. Popular with her classmates despite her plumpness, she knew she would be selected for certain parts. But she feared she would never land meaningful roles. She could see herself forever relegated to portraying incidental characters who rarely spoke a line.

Mari's mother, after hearing her anguish, wisely sought medical advice. The family doc-tor confirmed what her mom had thought: Mari, while heavier than average for her height and age, was not obese. The solution, the doctor told her, was neither severe dieting nor torturous bodybuilding. Rather, Mari should learn to moderate her intake of high-calorie foods, exercise more, and let her body proceed with the natural growing process.

Mari took home the health and nutrition materials the doctor provided and read them with genuine interest. She realized her weight was not a crisis at this point and, with a bit of discipline, she could bring it under control.

Now sixteen, Mari is in the high school drama club. She's 5 feet 5 inches (1.7 m) tall and weighs about 150 pounds (68 kg). While her body mass index (see chapter 5) charts her as slightly "at risk," weight-wise she's visibly in much better shape than she was three years earlier. A veteran actress with a number of rewarding credits in school and community productions, Mari still waits for that elusive lead—and she doesn't expect to be waiting forever.

WEIGHT CONTROL IS NO SIMPLE MATTER

Some of our ancestors were fat because they wanted to be. Some were lean, also because they wanted to be. Meanwhile, countless others discovered that weight and appearance were not easy to control. That's true today.

Researchers and doctors have learned much about nutritional needs and related problems. But basic medical advice about weight control today is little changed from the days of your great-great-grandparents. Robert Pool, in his book *Fat: Fighting the Obesity Epidemic,* remarks that as early as the 1930s, doctors understood the main nutritional factors. They "knew with great accuracy how much food a body needed daily to remain healthy—not just the number of calories, but also grams of protein, grams of carbohydrate, grams of fat, and the necessary trace amounts of various vitamins and minerals—and they were able to tell a patient precisely how many calories to cut from the normal daily intake to lose a pound, a pound and a half, or two pounds a week."[8]

Two questions should concern you: What's a healthy weight for me, and how do I maintain it? The lean and muscular body so desirable in modern society is, in fact, a healthy physical objective. Keeping yourself trim and strong will not necessarily result in a long, happy life, but it will probably help you resist and cope with illnesses and injuries. You may not be able to attain a fashion model's physique, though—and you don't need to. Different people the same age may vary in weight by 25 pounds (11 kg) or more and all be considered healthy. Likewise, children at the same height may be at markedly different, yet healthy, weights.[9]

Several key factors affect your healthy weight range. Doctors know now, for instance, that muscle tissue weighs more than fat tissue. Thus, if weight alone is used to determine the state of a person's health, a muscular individual might erroneously be considered as unhealthy as a fatty person of the same weight.

CHAPTER THREE

Why Are Americans Overweight?

TO MANY AMERICANS, THE
TRADITIONAL HABIT OF THREE
MEALS PER DAY IS MEANING-
LESS; THEY'RE EATING ALL
THE TIME.

W hy are Americans overweight? The short answer: Fatty foods taste good and exercise hurts. People like to eat; they don't particularly like to exercise. Those are natural instincts—and they can be killer instincts.

But those instincts aren't new. What makes your generation fatter than those who came before you? And what places certain population groups more at risk than others?

GOOD-TASTING FOOD CAN BE BAD

Processed fatty foods are convenient and afford-able even for low-income families. They're also more than a little tempting. It's these unhealthy foods, it seems, that capture most people's desires because they're tasty, cheap, and usually available within minutes.

Some of these foods are not completely bad. Along with their unhealthy ingredients, they con-tain nutrients your body can use. Others, however, offer little of nutritional value. They're treats— nothing more. It's OK to enjoy treats, as long as they aren't harmful. Sadly, a lot of the treats you and your friends devour today are definitely harmful.

Many soft drinks, for example, contain lots of sugar and almost nothing that contributes to your daily needs in minerals and vitamins. They're loaded with what nutritionists call empty calories.[1] They don't make you smart, they don't make you strong, they don't make you immune to diseases, but—if consumed in excess—they do make you fatter. It's been calculated that if you add one

12-ounce (340-ml) sugary soft drink per day to your food intake, you'll gain an extra pound in three to four weeks. This is in addition to the weight you're gaining normally as a growing teenager.

In *Underage & Overweight*, Frances M. Berg points out that weight problems can result not just from what and how much young people eat, but also from where and when they're eating it.[2] One example: Weight-conscious children might get into the habit of eating little or no breakfast, lunch, or even dinner—and then, unable to refrain any longer, they storm the kitchen just before bedtime. Another example: Some children, especially if they're unsupervised, basically engage in nonstop eating (snacks, then dinner, then more snacks) from the time they arrive home from school until the time they go to bed.

Doctor and author Stacy Ann Mitchell points out that the two reasons people eat—hunger and appetite—are not the same. "Hunger is the physical need for food . . . Appetite is a psychological need for food that has little, if anything, to do with the physical need for nutrition."[3] Among too many teenagers, appetite, not hunger, is controlling their physical development. Nutrition educator Sharron Dalton says that if she were to grade the overall diets of Americans in their early teens, most would receive a D or an F.[4]

Marshall's Story

By the time he entered ninth grade, Marshall weighed 190 pounds (86 kg) and stood 5 feet

6 inches (1.7 m) tall. He kept cookies stashed in different pockets of his book bag and candy bars in his school locker. His home was just four blocks from school, and he walked the distance—good exercise. Unhappily, he passed a fast-food restaurant on the way. His parents, always in a rush, gave him money to stop in for breakfast each morning and a snack each afternoon. Marshall invariably ordered the good stuff: a couple of ham and cheese biscuits with hash browns for breakfast, a hefty cheeseburger and jumbo fries later—all washed down with soft drinks.

When he got home, he wasn't really hungry, but munching chips or the current fad snack—accompanied by another soft drink— seemed natural while watching TV. He knew it wasn't healthy, but who cared? "I'm fat and I'm probably going to stay fat," he reasoned. "I might as well enjoy myself."

That changed when a physical exam revealed he had developed type 2 diabetes, a dangerous disease that once occurred mostly in adults. Not only did he need to bring his weight under control, the doctor told him, he needed to follow a careful diet and resist the extras. If he failed to get his act together, Marshall was warned, the consequences would be "unacceptable."

Supported by his family, Marshall did what he had to do. Breakfast now usually consists of bran cereal, and lunch is a wise selection of vegetables, fruits, pasta, and a *small portion of meat from the cafeteria. His walk to school detours around the fast-food stop. He walks two extra blocks each way while resisting taste-bud temptations. On fair days, he often roams for half an hour or longer, finding it an exhilarating way to unwind from classes. As he approaches high school graduation, Marshall still weighs 190 pounds (86 kg) but, having grown to 5 feet 11 inches (1.8 m), he's in much better health.*

TEMPTATIONS, TEMPTATIONS

Teenagers are bombarded by attractive advertisements for unhealthy foods. You're tempted to buy everything from sugar-rich cereals to greasy pizzas. The food industry pays an estimated $36 billion a year for advertisements.[5] The ads are obviously effective. By 2000, the public was spending some $110 billion annually for fast food (about four times more than the government spends for medical research).[6] Susan B. Roberts and Melvin B. Heyman, in their book *Feeding Your Child for Lifelong Health*, suggest to parents, "TV advertising is such a negative and powerful food influence that you may simply want to consider restricting your child's viewing to PBS and other noncommercial channels."[7]

If advertising isn't enough to lure customers, there are bonus incentives. Shoppers look for bargains, and all too often food bargains are fatty bargains.[8] Cheap fast food becomes even cheaper with two-for-the-price-of-one coupon offers. Free toys and other prizes are available from certain fast-food chains and cereal/snack sellers. Burger restaurants offer colorful play areas for young children. What youngster wouldn't be tempted?[9]

And of course, there's the convenience. For Americans living in or near cities and towns, the nearest fast-food eatery is just a short walk or drive away. Snack machines seem to be at every turn. Public libraries provide snack-laden lounges. Upscale bookstores offer browsers an aromatic island to lounge with a cup of cappuccino. Practically all automobiles today are designed with front and rear drink and food holders and disposal containers. Backpacks feature food and drink compartments. You're encouraged to snack while watching television and sports events, studying, riding in a car, hiking, and waiting for hair appointments and auto tune-ups. To many Americans, the traditional habit of three meals per day is meaningless; they're eating all the time.

Temptations confront you even at school. Many public schools sell greasy tacos, cheeseburgers, pizzas, and other fast-food items, in some cases supplied by brand-name restaurant chains.[10] Critics express alarm at the business arrangements convenience food and soft drink companies have forged with school systems and educational organizations. Aside from on-campus sales contracts, food corporations have funded educational programs and corporate executives have been given leadership roles in education-related institutions.[11] In their book *Generation Extra Large*, authors Lisa Tartamella, Elaine Herscher, and Chris Woolston observe that "in many schools, kids hear one message in class and see another in the lunch line. We teach them about nutrition and the importance of making good choices, yet we surround them with bad choices."[12]

At the same time students are being tempted by snacks, in many schools they're discouraged from good eating habits. Cafeteria menus include healthy but tasteless items. The interesting fare—à la carte pizza, burgers, fries—is far more popular. Hallway water fountains are often visibly grubby, prompting children to buy beverages from drink machines.[13]

In answering critics, the food industry has countered that tasty and convenient (and often fatty) foods are what consumers want. When they're offered healthier foods, vendors claim, buyers reject them.[14] If a food company advertises a low-fat item and it fails to sell, the company can't afford to continue marketing it. In order to remain in business, it has to offer products the public will buy. Thus, their most common products are tasty and attractive. To appeal to children who are bored with traditional breakfast fare, they add chocolate chips and fruit-flavored sugary delights to such products as microwave pancakes and breakfast cereals.[15]

It must be pointed out that not all fast food or processed food is bad for you. Certain sweet, tasty cereals, for example, can be part of a healthy diet. And along with the "junk" items, many fast-food restaurants serve healthy menu choices, including salads.[16] However, researchers doubt it's a complete coincidence that the explosion in obesity statistics has occurred at the same time as the explosion in fast-food popularity.

AMERICANS HAVE STOPPED MOVING

The second great contributor to obesity is lack of exercise. During the early 1960s, President John F. Kennedy stressed the need for physical fitness among Americans. Many school systems made PE class a daily requirement. By the turn of the century, though, other subjects had replaced phys ed as a priority. In her 2004 book *Rescuing the Emotional Lives of Overweight Children*, Dr. Sylvia Rimm reported that only one in three grade schools teach physical education.[17] Today, recognizing that obesity and a lack of exercise contribute to the nation's mounting health crisis, many educators are urging a reemphasis on physical education.

But basic health habits are formed at home. Some teenagers are even less active there than they are at school. They're glued to their seats for hours by their favorite TV shows, movies, the Internet, video games, and the phone. "Sedentary living appears to be a major factor in the accumulation of excess body fat," writes Frances M. Berg, "particularly for genetically vulnerable youth."[18]

On average, an American child watches television three to four hours every day.[19] Factoring in time spent with video games and computer entertainment, the average child spends five and a half hours per day—almost a fourth of her or his life—parked virtually motionless in front of a screen.[20] Two out of three children between the ages of eight and twelve have their own bedroom TV set; one out of three children from ages two to seven has a personal TV.[21] In the age before television, much more time during childhood development was spent on physical activity—either play or work.

Dr. Rimm points to research that suggests young people are even less physically active while watching TV than they are while reading a book. "Thus, television watching may be considered an 'extreme' sedentary activity that, when repeated over and over every day, leads to fewer calories burned and a steady climb in body weight."[22] Rimm observes that overweight children apply more time on average to the Internet, e-mail, and video games than children of healthy weight.[23]

Television can have another harmful effect on your weight and health. While you're sitting or lying dormant in front of the screen, you're being barraged with commercials that glorify foods and drinks high in calories but low in nutrients.

Television shouldn't be given a totally bad rap. It's an important tool that provides not just entertainment but educational services and vital information. Moreover, it's the viewer's personal lifestyle, not the inanimate television set, that contributes to obesity. Interestingly, health professionals point out that many children immerse themselves in television and other forms of inactive diversion in order to *escape* their weight-related depression.[24]

IS LIFE TOO EASY?

Life is indeed easy compared to a century ago. Overall, life for modern Americans is far more effortless—and thus more dangerous—than ever before. Everyday actions that required serious energy in past generations now are automated.

For example, students once walked considerable distances to and from school—5 miles (8 km) or more was not an unusual daily trudge. Most forms of entertainment, aside from reading and music, involved physical play. The workplace, much more commonly than now, was a place of *physical* work. Farmers of yesteryear labored with hand tools to grow and harvest crops; they didn't ride for hours on padded tractor seats. Laundry chores required "elbow grease"—not the setting of knobs on automatic washers and dryers. Your ancestors cut and sawed wood by hand, painted houses by hand, and mowed lawns with toilsome, engineless push cutters. They opened cans with manual twist devices and sharpened pencils with hand grinders. By comparison, Americans today, young and old, have become rather motionless.

Of course, if you're spending many hours each day sitting down, you can hardly be blamed. Schoolwork—especially in the computer age—requires just that. Nor can you be faulted for craving some downtime with television, the Internet, or video games. The old caution against all work and no play is as true today as ever before.

In the generations before electronic entertainment, though, a substantial portion of children's play was physical. For many youths today, very little of it is physical.

CHAPTER FOUR

Other Factors Linked to Obesity

[F]OR MOST OBESE INDIVIDUALS, MORE THAN ONE CAUSE IS INVOLVED.

I t's clear that bad eating habits should be discouraged and regular exercise should be encouraged. But for some people more than others, it's difficult to follow that advice. Circumstances beyond their control may present obstacles to healthy eating, healthy exercise, or both. Gluttony and laziness may not necessarily be the underlying culprits.

At the same time, researchers have found that these bad habits don't have the same effects on all young people. For example, among children the same age who consume similar varieties and quantities of food, some gain excess weight while others remain of average size.[1] Perhaps you've observed schoolmates who regularly devour enormous quantities of food but don't appear to grow very much, while others who seem to eat less get stouter year by year.

INFLUENCES OF FRIENDS AND FAMILY

As you grow, you're influenced by the behavior of your friends and classmates. This may include eating habits. Just as a youngster adopts the mannerisms and slang of those around her, explains Dr. Susan B. Roberts, "so she will also start to absorb their food habits, both good and bad."[2]

You're also influenced by family customs. One modern custom in particular seems to affect weight problems in a bad way: less than half of American families still eat dinner together regularly.[3] In her studies, Professor Sharron Dalton has found that "children raised in families who do not regularly prepare and eat family meals together are more likely to be overweight."[4]

Today, many youngsters arriving home after school find themselves alone, their parents at work. Some engage immediately in healthy exercise or homework. But that, unhappily, seems to be the exception. Few statistics are available to show in accurate detail how "home alone" children spend their hours after school.[5] To health professionals, however, it's obvious that with no supervision, many children indulge in overeating and excessive television viewing. The TV set is the afternoon baby-sitter, and physical "exercise" consists of trips from the sofa to the refrigerator and back.

You might face a nutrition challenge even when parents and other family members are around. In some families, everybody overeats. They consume unhealthy foods without thinking. In many situations, bring-home fast food or pizza deliveries are common dining fare. Otherwise, they indulge in convenience dinners—processed, packaged meals that can be heated in the microwave oven and placed on the table in a few minutes.[6] Children are given soft drinks as their mealtime beverage—and the refrigerator and pantry are well stocked with sodas for between-meal enjoyment. In short, these children are raised with little concern for healthy eating habits. Dr. Rimm refers to such families as "Happy Heavies."[7]

In some homes, parents sporadically attempt to impose healthy eating habits. They might

require you—for a while—to eat at least one of
your vegetables before dessert is allowed. But
unless you're made to understand *why* certain
foods are very important and others can lead to
problems, this occasional diet policing can back-
fire: It can make you resent healthy foods.[8]

Dalton agrees with many other health professionals that "family behaviors and interactions
undoubtedly contribute greatly to childhood obesity." She points out, though, that other factors
may be involved.[9]

LOW INCOMES, HIGH CALORIES

According to various studies, nonwhite children
have the highest obesity rates. Among minority
and low-income populations in certain areas of
the country, as many as half the young people
are considered overweight.[10] The most recent
National Health and Nutrition Examination Study
(NHANES) found that 29 percent of white boys
ages six to eleven are overweight or at risk of
becoming overweight. In comparison, 36 percent
of black boys in that age range are overweight or
at risk, and 43 percent of Mexican American boys
are. Among girls ages six to eleven, the percentages were notably different—although, again,
nonwhites are at the greatest risk. Specifically,
the NHANES study found 23 percent of white
girls, 35 percent of Mexican American girls, and
38 percent of African American girls are overweight or at risk.[11]

Native American children fare at least as badly. By one account, 39 percent of American Indian youngsters are overweight.[12]

"Gender, culture, and discrimination all play a role," Dalton writes. "But however you approach it, the statistics are clear: children from low-income and less-educated families have a much greater risk of obesity."[13] That conclusion was reinforced by the results of several studies conducted from 1971 to 2004; they indicated that the percentage of overweight children ages fifteen to seventeen is twice as great among poor families as among those who are more affluent.[14]

Reasons for this greater risk are varied. For one thing, exercise is not so simple for children in many low-income communities. Parents have expressed worry that their neighborhoods are unsafe for outdoor play, so they keep their children indoors almost all the time. "Kids who are not allowed to run outside and play are left with few alternatives but to sit around indoors," Dalton summarizes.[15]

Researchers have also found that certain ethnic and cultural backgrounds affect how young people and their parents think of weight and body dimensions. Different peoples and communities have different views of what is an attractive, desirable size.[16] Dalton observes, for instance, that "Hispanic women are generally admired for larger hips and generous body size."[17] She adds, "In predominantly black or Latino neighborhoods, obesity is becoming the norm rather than the exception because of the combined forces that promote fatness among people living there."[18] As one health worker puts it, "When everyone in the neighborhood is big, big is normal."[19]

Not surprisingly, the incidence of obesity-related diseases is higher among these groups. Type 2 diabetes, for example, is most prevalent among low-income populations. Almost 50 percent of the Pima people of Arizona have been found to have type 2 diabetes.[20] In his book *Fat: Fighting the Obesity Epidemic*, Robert Pool observes that fatty dietary habits and inadequate exercise were the "immediate cause" of obesity among the Pima. But he points out that the Pima weren't always over-weight. It may not be a coincidence, he suggested, that after World War II, the Pima culture and environment shifted "from traditional Indian to modern Western."[21]

Health researchers almost universally agree that obesity is a problem for all population groups. "There is no doubt," writes Dr. Rimm, "that obesity is at epidemic levels in almost all age and ethnic groups in America, yet we still have not been able to stop or even slow the rise in obesity rates."[22]

THE QUESTION OF HEREDITY

Many adults of average or below-average weight are amused to review their baby pictures, which depict decidedly plump infants. Quite often, infant fat disappears as a child becomes an energetic toddler. Even if the child appears fat entering the teen years, it is not necessarily a cause for alarm. People who are overweight as children do not necessarily grow to become fat adults.

There is a tendency, however, for weight patterns to continue from adolescence into adulthood.[23] One survey examined children from age two to seventeen and followed up on their health seventeen years later. Interestingly, it found that 77 percent of children who were overweight at the beginning of the project remained overweight as adults. Meanwhile, fewer than 10 percent of the children who were of normal weight at the beginning grew into overweight adults.[24]

Are these long-term patterns determined by family lifestyle factors? Or could they indicate that you *inherit* your relative body size?

Medical researchers have found the issue of hereditary obesity to be complex. Many studies have shown that children who have overweight parents tend to be overweight themselves. One statistic is that if both your parents are obese, you have an 80 percent likelihood of becoming obese; if one of your parents is obese, you have a 40 percent likelihood of becoming obese; if neither of your parents is obese, your likelihood of becoming obese is slight—about 3 percent.

But does this prove that "fat genes" are passed along from adults to children? Or does it merely indicate that children are likely to become fat if they grow up in homes where fatty foods are the standard fare of their parents, and where exercise is discouraged? "Show me the food intake of a child," writes Dr. Fred Pescatore in his book *Feed Your Kids Well,* "and I will show you the dietary and health problems that child will have as an adult."[25]

Not all children whose parents are obese will become obese themselves. Likewise, some children struggle with obesity in spite of the fact that they have parents of thin or average build. Brothers and sisters in many families prefer different types of foods and develop different eating and exercise habits. A girl may have a sweet tooth while her brother loves vegetables and salads, or vice-versa.[26]

In past generations, most doctors concluded that children became overweight mainly because of their parenting and home situations. Since 1994, discoveries in genetic research have strengthened the theory that a child's weight might be affected by hereditary factors. Several types of genes have been identified that could affect weight.[27] But while heredity can play a role in a family's weight patterns, scientists believe, so can shared behavior among family members. That is, close relatives typically share identical or similar habits of eating and exercise.[28]

Dalton points out that it's "exceedingly difficult" to know how significant heredity is to obesity because "biological and environmental factors are so tightly intertwined . . . It is not a matter of genes *or* environment or of genes *versus* environment, but of genes *and* environment that act when a person becomes fat."[29] She adds that some children seem to be more vulnerable to obesity than others.[30]

Regardless of hereditary or shared behavior factors, obesity can be conquered. The fact that other members of your household are on the road to obesity doesn't mean you're required to join them. "If both parent and child can change their diet and exercise habits together," Rimm believes, "they can overcome the effect of genetics on body weight."[31]

ADDITIONAL CONTRIBUTING FACTORS

Many young people turn to food, even when they aren't hungry, to cope with stress. You undoubtedly encounter stress in a variety of forms yourself: pressure to complete a school project, criticism or taunting, grades, relationship problems involving friends or relatives, uncertainty about your future. Even loneliness can be stressful. Rimm points out that there is a "connection between loneliness and overeating."[32]

Health problems not directly related to your weight can nevertheless affect it. If you have asthma, for instance, you may be limited in the forms and frequency of exercise you can enjoy.[33] If a broken limb puts you in a cast for weeks or months, it isn't uncommon to gain extra weight during that time—weight that may not be easy to lose or to absorb into your natural growth progression.

Scientists are investigating the possibility that certain viruses cause or contribute to weight problems. Recent studies have indicated three separate viruses may be linked to obesity in animals. Can such viruses affect the weight of humans? If so, it raises the frightening prospect that obesity might be contagious. For the moment, no conclusive evidence has been found.[34]

In their book *The Overweight Child: Promoting Fitness and Self-Esteem*, Teresa Pitman and Miriam Kaufman explain that for most obese individuals, more than one cause is involved. They also acknowledge that "we don't really know why some people weigh more than others of the same height and frame." Human weight, they write, is "a very complex subject."[35]

CHAPTER FIVE

Medical Professionals Chart the Situation

YOUR WEIGHT ALONE DOES NOT DETERMINE WHETHER YOU ARE OBESE. WEIGHT MUST BE CONSIDERED IN RELATION TO SUCH OTHER FACTORS AS HEIGHT, AGE, AND RATE OF GROWTH.

America is a world leader in obesity rates. Researchers agree that this stems mainly from the fact that it is a comparatively affluent country. But gradually, people in less advanced countries are adopting the same style of living. While obesity rates in the United States have tripled during the past half century, in China they have quadrupled, according to the World Health Organization (WHO). The WHO believes one of the new century's major health challenges is "the global spread of diet-linked disease."[1]

Contributing factors in the global obesity crisis may differ somewhat from country to country, but the fundamental causes—too much fatty food and diminished exercise—are universal. Let's see what medical professionals tell us about human body types and how food affects our size and general health.

WHAT'S A "NORMAL" WEIGHT?

People commonly describe themselves as normal, thin, or fat. But there are different shades of normal, thin, and fat. A muscular athlete might be 6 feet (1.8 m) tall, weigh 220 pounds (100 kg), and be considered normal in weight and build. A non-athlete who's 6 feet tall and weighs 220 pounds, whose weight consists mainly of fat tissue rather than muscle tissue, cannot join the athlete in the "normal" category.

Your weight alone does not determine whether you are obese. Weight must be considered in relation to such other factors as height, age, and rate of growth. Doctors are particularly careful in diagnosing weight concerns with juvenile patients. If parents are alarmed, they may impose dramatic eating changes not just on that child but on the entire family, resulting in poor nutrition for everyone.[2]

The first growth charts for determining appropriate weight levels came out in the 1970s. In 2000, the Centers for Disease Control and Prevention (CDC), an agency within the U.S. Department of Health and Human Services (HHS), introduced more accurate charts. These charts reflected what had become known as the body mass index, or BMI.

The BMI is a mathematical formula: your weight (in kilograms) divided by the square of your height (in meters). The measurements can easily be converted to pounds and inches. To quickly calculate your BMI in pounds and inches, use this formula:

1. Compute the square of your height (multiply your height times itself) in inches.
2. Multiply your weight in pounds by 703.
3. Divide the weight result by the height result.

Sample results: If you are 5 feet (60 inches) tall and weigh 112 pounds, your BMI is approximately 22. Whether this is a low, average, or high weight depends on your age, sex, and other factors. A BMI of 23 or higher, for instance, indicates a

weight problem for a girl at age 10. By the time
she's 16, however, the same BMI suggests no
problem—in fact, at that age, she could register a
BMI of 28 and be considered only "borderline" in
terms of overweight risk.[3] An average BMI for a
child in the first grade is approximately 16. An
average BMI for a high school senior is approximately 22.

Doctors chart the BMI in relation to your age.
Different charts are used for boys and girls.
Depending on your chart placement, you can be
classed as underweight, average, or overweight. If
your BMI ranks in the ninety-fifth percentile or
above, you're considered overweight. If it falls in
the range of the eighty-fifth to ninety-fourth percentile, you're said to be "at risk" of developing an
excess weight problem.

Sharron Dalton points out that the BMI is
not a perfect tool for determining a person's
desirable weight.[4] (Health officials have stopped
using the term "ideal weight."[5]) Dalton empha-
sizes that "the BMI and corresponding growth
charts don't show the whole picture." She says
results may vary from child to child, for complex
reasons.[6] Dalton adds that the BMI does not take
growth rate into account. "BMI is only a guide-
line," she says. "It does not measure bone, fat,
or muscle."[7]

Growth charts, a BMI calculator, and explana-
tory information can be found at the Web site of
the CDC: http://www.cdc.gov/nccdphp/dnpa/
bmi/childrens_BMI/about_childrens_BMI.htm.

Many experts believe mild examples of excess fat don't notably endanger a person's health. One study has suggested that a forty-five-year-old man at 20 percent above his "ideal weight" has his life expectancy only a few months shorter than "healthy" men his age. Moderately overweight women are believed to be less at risk than men.[8]

Where excess weight is distributed around your body, however, could be a significant factor in how seriously your health is at risk. For example, many females fret over unattractive figures caused by fatty thighs and hips.[9] More dangerous, though, is massive fat around the middle to upper body, surrounding the vital organs.

SEPARATING FAT FROM FAT

Regardless of your BMI rating, you need to be aware that your body weight and what it means to your overall health are complex matters. A nagging problem with efforts to address the obesity problem has been incomplete and sometimes faulty information about what causes it. For example, after nutritionists cited saturated fats as a health culprit in the latter half of the twentieth century, food companies began reducing saturated fat content in their products. In many cases, they substituted trans fats—which were soon pronounced to be more harmful than saturated fats.[10]

Many people assume that all fat is bad. The reality is that a body *needs* a certain amount of fat to function. It's a primary source of energy. It's vital to cell composition and to your chemical makeup. "If it weren't for fat," Dr. Fred Pescatore says, "our bodies would disintegrate and fall apart."[11]

The same is true with cholesterol—another word that raises health alarms, especially among overweight people. Too much of the wrong kind of cholesterol in the bloodstream clogs the arteries. But again, just as there are good and bad fats, there are good and bad forms of cholesterol.[12]

Sharron Dalton notes that all types of fats—mono fats, poly fats, saturated fats, and trans fats—by definition are "fattening." Some, however, are necessary for good health while others are harmful.[13]

The type of fat heavily criticized for its role in obesity is trans fat. Scientists have found that excessive consumption of trans fats can build up cholesterol in the blood and lead to heart disease. Nutritionists suggest that trans fats and saturated fats should account for less than 10 percent of the calories you consume, but many Americans double that amount.[14] Various packaged desserts, french fries, potato chips, greasy burgers, and pastries are high in trans fat content. Fast food restaurants in particular have come under fire for the levels of trans fat contained in their fries.[15]

Sweetened, carbonated soft drinks are another primary target in the anti-obesity war because they are high in nonessential sugar content. The average American drinks about twice as much soda today as in the 1980s. Among children ages six to eleven, almost half drink about 15 ounces (425 ml) of carbonated beverages daily.[16] It's estimated that if a middle-school-aged girl adds a regular 12-ounce soda (340 ml; about 145 calories) to her daily food consumption, that alone will increase her weight by 12 to 15 pounds (5–7 kg) in a year. (This assumes that she makes no other changes in her eating and exercise routines.)[17]

DIETARY GUIDELINES FOR AMERICANS

The federal government's MyPyramid (formerly known as the Food Pyramid) is a general guide to what kinds of foods (and how much of them) you should eat in addition to obtaining daily physical exercise. It was developed by the U.S. Department of Agriculture (USDA) and the HHS and is based on the Dietary Guidelines for Americans, which are updated every five years. The USDA and HHS realized that one size does not fit all and that the ideal amount of food intake differs depending on a person's age, gender, and daily activities. In 2005, they provided a Web site, http://www.mypyramid.gov, which includes an interactive food guidance system and which customizes a healthy eating and exercise plan for each individual. The MyPyramid symbol on the site adds physical activity as "steps to a healthier you" to the eating plan. The steps and the person climbing them represent the significance of physical activity every day.

The pyramid symbol shows colorful vertical slices or bands to indicate generally the comparative amounts of the six food groups you should include in your daily diet. The varying widths of the slices represent how much food you can choose from each group and is to be used as a guide rather than as exact amounts. The narrowing of each food group slice from bottom to top stands for eating foods in moderation. The foods at the base, where the pyramid is widest, are those foods with little or no solid fats or added sugars. These foods should be chosen more often. The six colored slices represent the six food groups, and show that food from all the groups are needed daily for a healthy life. The orange slice, the widest band, represents the grains group; the green slice is the vegetable group; the blue slice is the milk, yogurt, and cheese group; the red slice represents the fruit group; the purple slice indicates the meat and bean group; and the yellow slice represents oils, such as vegetable oils, nuts, and avocados. On the site's "Inside the Pyramid" page (http://www.mypyramid.gov/pyramid/index.html), when you click on one of the slices, you're shown common examples of the foods in that group and advice on which ones are considered best to eat.

Some medical professionals have discredited the USDA dietary guidelines. Among other concerns, they challenge the value of bread and pasta as part of the recommended food foundation.

Others believe that the pyramid plan or model
might be improved (for example, by differentiat-
ing healthy from unhealthy carbohydrates),
but that it is an invaluable guide for weight
management.[18]

Nutritionists explain that people can satisfy their
hunger by filling up with various kinds of foods
represented in the pyramid. Unhappily, many
Americans choose poorly. You can help control
your weight by paying attention to the "calorie
density" of each food type.[19] Simply put: don't fill
up on foods high in calories. Instead, satisfy your
hunger by consuming more high-fiber foods, vegetables, and fruits. As for liquids, water is obviously
a smarter selection than soft drinks.

HOW DO YOU EAT?

Your weight can be affected not only by what
you eat but how you eat it. How fast you consume a meal is important. Americans often eat
in a hurry. Some children often dash to the
kitchen for a blitz dinner during the long com-
mercial break between television shows. At
school, twelve to fifteen minutes is the average
actual eating time at lunch periods.[20] Parents
commonly remark that their children "inhale"
their meals.

Among the problems with rapid eating is that
you're ignoring your natural signals regarding
appetite. Your stomach will tell you when it's
full—if you pay attention. A time-honored piece of

dining advice is to put down your fork between bites. If you're really hungry for another bite, then take one. If not, don't. While rushing to cram down food, you don't realize you've stuffed yourself until the deed is done.[21]

Nutritionists in the past disapproved of between-meal eating. Today, many health professionals advise it. In their book *Fueling the Teen Machine*, Ellen Shanley and Colleen Thompson remark that for teenagers, healthy between-meal snacks actually are important. "You need to keep that engine running." It's imperative that the snacks be nutritious, not junk food. Shanley and Thompson suggest such choices as yogurt, fruit, granola bars, pretzels, cereal, and veggies with dip. Cookies and milk, milkshakes, chips, peanut butter, and other flavorful snacks should be consumed only in limited portions. "A 10-ounce [284-milligram] bag of chips," for example, "is *too much*!" they assert. Quantity in relation to the amount of exercise you get is a key equation. "The more active you are, the more calories you need. The reverse is also true."[22]

Bear in mind that small changes in eating habits can lead to weight problems. Suppose you're of average weight and have been following reasonably healthy eating habits. Then you acquire a taste for a certain treat that adds about 100 calories per day to your food consumption. As a consequence, you can expect to gain about 10 pounds (4.5 kg) in a year *in addition to* the natural weight gain of a growing teenager.[23]

MYTHS AND FACTS ABOUT OBESITY

When it comes to obesity, it is sometimes challenging to distinguish fact from fiction. The following myths and the facts that dispel them may help to set the record straight.

Myth: "Obesity runs in my family; there's nothing I can do about it."

Fact: Family lifestyles affect food consumption and weight issues; heredity may be a factor for some individuals as well. In either case, obesity can be prevented, and persons who are already obese can find solutions to their problem.

Myth: Although a few young people are obviously overweight, most are relatively healthy eaters and have little to worry about.

Fact: More than 90 percent of American teenagers and preteens consume excessive levels of saturated fat. More than 80 percent consume excessive levels of total fat.[24]

Myth: Healthy foods include potato chips (a vegetable) and pizza loaded with cheese (a dairy item).

Fact: Along with their vegetable and dairy nutrients, most varieties of chips and pizza give you high measures of fat.

Myth: You can eat all you want in any given sitting and then correct that eating orgy by skipping your next meal (or two).

Fact: Roller-coaster eating habits can open a Pandora's box of health problems. These range from nutritional imbalances to bingeing and purging and other dangerous dietary patterns.

Myth: Once you learn to accept yourself for who you are, there's really nothing wrong with being overweight.

Fact: It's true that your appearance should not diminish your self-esteem. You should know, however, that more than 300,000 American deaths each year can be attributed to eating and activity habits. Eating and exercise patterns are linked to heart and circulatory problems, diabetes, certain types of cancer, bone and joint problems, and other very real ailments.

Myth: Type 2 diabetes is caused by eating too much sugar.

Fact: Type 2 diabetes comes about because of insulin resistance to excessive fat. Excessive fat can result not only from eating too much sugar but also from eating too many french fries, potato chips, fatty burgers, and other unwholesome foods.[25]

Myth: "I know I'm fat—but I'll grow out of it naturally."

Fact: Adolescents who are overweight face a 77 percent likelihood of becoming overweight adults.

Myth: Some diets obviously work. Those fantastic weight-loss testimonials can't all be frauds.

Fact: Countless individuals have achieved astonishing weight reduction using any of a number of diet programs. But the great majority of dieters fail to keep off the weight. Weight control in most situations requires long-term changes in lifestyle.

IS OBESITY A DISEASE?

Some professionals regard obesity as a physical condition that results from lax personal behavior. The authors of *Livin' Large*, among others, describe it as a disease. A number of health-related and federal organizations likewise classify it as a disease. They include the American Obesity Association, the National Institutes of Health, the American Dietetic Association, and the Internal Revenue Service. On the other hand, the federal government's Medicare and Medicaid programs don't consider it a disease in itself—although it can be *related* to recognized diseases. Regardless, health professionals believe that most overweight people can, if they try, reduce their weight and thus improve their health.

Sharron Dalton writes that "obesity is *not* a disease, though it is clearly related to diseases such as diabetes and hypertension . . . Most obese individuals suffer not from a physical or mental illness, but from *a condition of immoderation.* Overweight children and adults need a balanced lifestyle informed by healthy food and activity choices."[26]

CHAPTER SIX

Problems Caused by Excessive Weight

In extreme cases, obesity and related health problems can reduce a youngster's life expectancy by as much as twenty years.

Y ou, a member of your family, or perhaps a friend could be living under a dangerous delusion about the issue of excessive weight. You may be thinking, "So what if I'm a little heavy . . . or even a lot? As long as I'm happy, what's the harm? I have a whole lifetime ahead of me to slim down."

It's true obesity in adulthood brings greater health risks than in childhood. But a number of ailments are associated with juvenile obesity as well. In children, common weight-related problems are labored breathing, strained joints, and high blood pressure.[1] One doctor has observed that obese children experience some of the same physical difficulties as people in old age. Literally, "they have trouble moving."[2] Excessive weight can cause you psychological woes, too.

HEART AND CIRCULATION DISEASES

Heart ailments and problems with the cardiovascular system are growing among young people. These include heart attacks, strokes, hypertension, and artery problems. Risks increase as you pass through your teens into young adulthood. A 2002 government report showed that among Americans ages fifteen through thirty-four, the rate of death by heart disease had increased by 10 percent over the period of a decade. Obesity is considered a primary reason.[3] Even children in their early teens are beginning to show symptoms of heart disease—a phenomenon almost unheard of in previous generations of youngsters.[4]

These types of physical conditions are made much worse by a lack of exercise. Doctors point out that physical fitness not only reduces the risk of heart attacks and strokes; it improves mental functions.[5] That's because exercise stimulates the circulatory system. Clogged arteries diminish the blood flow to the brain.

DIABETES

One in five deaths among Americans older than twenty-five is brought about by diabetes.[6] Various types of diabetes have different causes. Type 2 diabetes, previously a disease suffered almost exclusively by adults, increasingly is diagnosed in children. It begins with a buildup of glucose, a form of sugar, in the blood. To a great extent, this results from an overconsumption of foods high in carbohydrates. The pancreas reacts to the excess glucose by releasing more insulin into the bloodstream. Over time, imbalances in blood sugar and insulin cause damage to vital organs and to the eyes and blood vessels. It can lead to blindness. Circulation problems can sometimes result in the loss of toes and feet and ultimately in premature death.

Most people with type 2 diabetes are over-weight. By exercising properly and shedding surplus fat, they can lessen the symptoms and learn to manage the disease to some extent.[7]

IMPAIRED BREATHING

When fat tissue presses against your breathing passage, a variety of problems can result. Drowsiness results from the reduced oxygen supply to the bloodstream. Sleep apnea is a condition in which normal breathing literally stops for a few moments until the brain reacts to "jumpstart" the respiratory system. Although sufferers may not realize it, they wake up repeatedly during the night, gasping for breath. Once common only in adults, apnea is being diagnosed increasingly in overweight children. In most cases, apnea takes its toll over a period of years. Interrupted sleep at night leads to a plethora of unhealthy daytime exertions and distractions. If the brain doesn't respond in time to the halted breathing, apnea itself can be fatal.

Other kinds of breathing ailments may be complicated by obesity. Children with asthma have greater difficulties coping with their disease if they are grossly overweight. They typically require more medication and medical attention.

OTHER MEDICAL CONCERNS

Obesity can hasten your sexual maturity, which heightens emotional and psychological problems during your years of development. Obese girls may experience menstrual irregularity. Obesity also can contribute to teenagers' acne problems and other skin conditions.[8]

Fat tissue in some individuals literally applies pressure to the brain. Headaches that result from this type of pressure, not surprisingly, are far more common in overweight individuals.[9]

Although not a significant danger for children, certain types of cancer have been associated with long-term obesity. Few Americans (just 8 percent, according to an American Cancer Society survey) are aware of the potential obesity-cancer connection. However, one study by the American Cancer Society indicated the risk of cancer among obese women is 55 percent higher than among women of normal weight. Obese men, according to the research, were 33 percent more at risk than men of average dimensions.[10] Remember that obesity trends often begin while you're young.

Unnatural weight strains the hips, knees, and feet, and can lead to osteoarthritis. Even at a young age, overweight individuals suffer from the effects. Studies have suggested females who are overweight for a period of twenty-five years are three times more likely to need hip replacements in later life than other women.[11]

The liver controls harmful substances that circulate through our bodies. Liver disease is commonly linked to alcohol or other forms of substance abuse—but it also can be brought on by excess fat.[12] At the same time, some of the diets adopted by weight-conscious individuals present imbalances to normal nutrition. This complicates the task of the liver. In general, dietary imbalances—which result from overeating certain types of foods while avoiding others—can cause unexpected, long-term problems.

SOCIAL AND PSYCHOLOGICAL ISSUES

If you're conspicuously overweight, you know the hurtful nature of the "size prejudice" you encounter from your peers. Observers tend to attach negative personal characteristics to people who are overweight. They might assume, for example, that the individual is lazy, slow, sloppy, and ignorant of basic health concerns.[13]

Television journalist Al Roker, who battled weight prejudice as a youngster, notes that "many movies, television shows, and cartoons go for the cheap laugh by making fun of fat people."[14] Many children simply take the hits. Others try to conceal their weight, perhaps by wearing long, baggy clothes—even in summertime. They prefer to cope with the discomfort of overdressing rather than expose unattractive bodies.

Some pediatricians consider psychosocial stress to be the most damaging element of juvenile obesity.[15] It can lead to depression, which presents varied potential dangers not directly related to weight—substance abuse, for example. Obese children generally have low self-esteem and, in some cases, come to hate their bodies. They frequently describe themselves as sad, lonely, afraid, and different. Boys are often dismayed that they lack athletic abilities. Heavy girls focus more on their unattractive appearance.[16] Dr. Susan Roberts says children—especially girls—begin to compare their body dimensions to those of their friends before they start grade school. "Maybe she will come home from a play date one day and say, 'Mom, my tummy sticks out,' or 'Daddy, am I fat?'"[17]

Plump individuals often take comfort in eating, which worsens their condition. Rimm notes that stress contributes to appetite problems. "Stress causes serotonin levels in the blood to decrease, which then causes craving for carbohydrates. Foods rich in carbohydrates, those sweets that children turn to for comfort, raise serotonin levels and cause sad children to feel better, at least temporarily. Yet those carbs increase heavy children's weight problems and perpetuate their emotional crises."[18]

Negative feelings about weight during childhood can affect your future hopes and plans.[19] In surveying children on topics concerning the future, Rimm found that very overweight youngsters were three times as likely to be worried as average-weight children.[20] Weight problems, she says, seemed to influence children's future expectations and goals.[21]

Your academic performance can suffer as a result of weight concerns. Rimm notes that exceptionally overweight children are twice as likely to be found in ADD (attention deficit disorder) programs. Meanwhile, Rimm has observed that gifted and talented programs include a smaller percentage of children who are excessively heavy.[22]

Feelings of inferiority or nonacceptance can be felt at home—the very place where children should expect comfort and shelter from ridicule. Rimm reports she has found "very overweight" boys and girls to be three to four times more likely to complain of poor relationships with other family members.[23]

Overall, it can result in a tragic cycle. Countless obese youngsters have tried repeatedly and unsuccessfully to bring their weight under control. They conclude that even if they exercise and give up fatty foods, they'll never be thin, "attractive," and accepted. Frustrated, they take what comfort they can from the television set and the refrigerator.[24]

SOCIETY PAYS A HIGH PRICE

Rising health care costs and demands on the system make obesity a problem society and its government must face. A U.S. government report in 2000 estimated obesity and excess weight and their related problems were costing the country $117 billion per year.[25] Those costs are ultimately borne by the public through taxes and health insurance premiums.

U.S. surgeon general Richard Carmona pointed out that obesity poses a national security risk as well as health and economic woes. "Our preparedness as a nation depends on our health as individuals," he stated at a 2003 national conference on juvenile obesity.[26]

The immediate toll, though, is borne by individuals. The somber bottom line, Sharron Dalton writes, is that "an obese child can expect a shorter life." In extreme cases, obesity and related health problems can reduce a youngster's life expectancy by as much as twenty years.[27]

CHAPTER SEVEN

Conquering Obesity

DEVELOP A COLLABORATIVE APPROACH THAT INVOLVES YOUR PARENTS AND OTHER MEMBERS OF YOUR FAMILY.

I f you're overweight and you've tried in vain to reduce, you understand the difficulty. It's one thing for a doctor, teacher, parent, or friend to admonish _ to eat less and exercise more. It's quite anothe :o succeec in doing what's necessary.

But you can. Many nutrition educators point out that although obesity is one of the gravest health problems facing the country, it also is preventable.[1]

WHERE TO START?

You'll need support, and ideally, you'll find your support foundation at home. Good health habits actually should begin in early childhood. Dr. Susan B. Roberts, a nutrition researcher, educator, and author, advises parents, "When you introduce your child to healthy foods in the right ways, she learns to actually enjoy the foods that are best for her development and long-term good health. . . . So if your young child learns to enjoy vegetables for dinner every night and fresh fruit for dessert, she incorporates these healthy foods into her developing subconscious blueprint for what a proper meal should be. Not only does it taste good to her, it feels right, too."[2]

Older children and adults, of course, have different food requirements than young children. That's why nutrition education is essential for both parents and children.[3] If you're an overweight teenager, perhaps neither you nor your parents have learned dietary basics. Or you might understand the basics but choose to ignore them. In either case, begin by examining them carefully—and taking them very seriously.

Develop a collaborative approach that involves your parents and other members of your family. (All family members, including those who aren't struggling with weight concerns, can benefit from a healthier home environment.) If a parent is making a serious attempt to establish good diet and exercise patterns for the family, don't resist—join the cause. Psychologists suggest that in some home settings, parents should be more responsible for what their children eat and should not be afraid to set limitations.[4] Dr. Fred Pescatore, an advocate of low-carb eating, writes that in formulating a dietary plan, parents and children alike should be involved.[5]

A SENSIBLE APPROACH TO EATING

Ellen Shanley and Colleen Thompson, in their book *Fueling the Teen Machine*, recommend a simple formula for basic teen health: Engage in daily physical activity and follow a general diet of healthy foods—specifically, one that is "low in saturated fat and cholesterol and moderate in total fat."[6] Be wary of foods and drinks that are exceptionally high in sugar and salt content. Remember, you have a choice. "If you choose sensibly, you greatly increase your chances of leading a healthy, productive, and active life."[7]

Dieticians do not insist you avoid potentially harmful foods altogether. Unless you have a medical condition that mandates a very strict diet, a cheeseburger, cake, soft drinks, potato chips, candy, and ice cream can be enjoyed occasionally without guilt. But treat those as treats—they certainly aren't required eating. What's required is the combination of food types described in the MyPyramid plan. From day to day, meal to meal, satisfy your appetite with the recommended products, not with the junk.

Equally important: *Learn when to stop!* Eat (healthy foods) if you're hungry; don't eat if you aren't.

Between-meal snacks aren't forbidden. But keep the refrigerator stocked with fruits and veggies instead of unhealthy snacks.[8] When you go on a trip, take along smart snack choices such as apples and other fruits. At travel stops, you're likely to be lured by snack and drink machines tempting you with products of questionable nutritional value. Avoid the temptation by providing your own weight-wise snacks.

Juveniles should shun alcoholic beverages, of course, and consume high-caffeine products only in careful moderation. Bear in mind that a teenager is not an adult. What some adults might regard as "light" alcohol consumption can be ruinous to adolescents. Just because a parent "needs" two or three cups of coffee every morning and doesn't seem to suffer ill effects doesn't mean it's all right for you. Most doctors will tell you caffeine is a bad habit for adults and worse for juveniles. Excessive caffeine—which also is contained in many soft drinks—can damage the kidneys, nervous system, and developing bones. Both alcohol and caffeine can become addictive.[9]

A SENSIBLE APPROACH TO EXERCISE

Exercise is essential to good health. "Along with diet," Dr. Sylvia Rimm tells parents, "it is the most fundamental way to help your child move toward a healthy weight and overcome any genetic disposition he may have toward gaining weight."[10] She cites one survey that showed women lost 7 percent of their midsection fat in a year simply by committing to a daily walking regimen; they didn't change their eating habits or resort to exhaustive exercise.[11]

Dr. Fred Pescatore explains that exercise serves two physical purposes: It increases strength (building muscle cells) and heightens aerobic activity. Aerobic stimulation, among other benefits, helps the body's immune system ward off illnesses.[12]

Exercise can take many forms—most of which can be enjoyable, if practiced in moderation. Just a few examples are the following: shooting hoops on a backyard or neighborhood court; dancing; walking or running for a mile or so a day; jumping rope; playing softball, volleyball, or touch football; or riding a bicycle. Identify a form of exercise that involves other people, if possible. Researchers have found that most youngsters aren't likely to exercise much unless it's entertaining and they have someone with whom to play.[13] Whatever your interests, you almost certainly can find a pleasant, rewarding form of exercise and companions to join you in the fun.

Probably the major distraction vying for your exercise time is television. Studies repeatedly indicate juvenile obesity rates are highest among those children who spend the most time watching TV.[14] Health professionals have numerous suggestions for controlling the TV habit. For example, turn off the TV at family mealtimes. Arrange your TV viewing situation so that at least some of your viewing time can include physical exercise (watch TV or listen to music while working out on a treadmill or exercise bike). Limit combined TV viewing and computer entertainment time to two hours per day. For every hour you spend Web surfing or watching TV, spend at least half an hour in some form of physical exercise. Preteens and teenagers, it's been recommended, should engage in some form of physical exercise for at least an hour every day.[15]

Research has suggested that the simple procedure of reducing TV time from three hours per day to one could diminish the risk of obesity substantially. In reality, Rimm says, most overweight youngsters indulge in TV more than three hours per day.[16] The connection between television and obesity is obvious, she believes. "A study of 2,971 youths between ages eight and sixteen found that girls who watched four or more hours of television a day were more likely to be overweight than those who watched less than four hours."[17] Other studies have verified the connection between excessive TV viewing and excessive weight.[18]

There's a negative, weight-related side effect. Children usually aren't completely "inactive" while watching TV—they're munching. One study has reported the average American child consumes 600 calories while watching TV each day.[19]

A SENSIBLE NEW LIFESTYLE

A combination of changes in your daily routines can help you reduce and control your weight. Again, changes should begin at home. Many advisers, including Rimm, advocate family activities for improved health. Not only is it good for the weight; it's good for the mind and emotions. "From board and card games to backyard baseball and hula hoops, the family that plays together cements a bond that preserves family relationships," Rimm explains. "Actively playing together rather than merely observing a screen or only passing one another on the way to work or meetings establishes an empowering family relationship."[20]

Psychologists observe that not only do many American families neglect to eat full, healthy meals together; they rarely exercise together, either. A few hours every week of family walking, bike riding, or backyard activities could be time well spent in many respects. While providing vital exercise, it would give children relaxing opportunities to share their problems and interests and to vent frustration.

If family activity opportunities seldom arise, chart a personal course to a better lifestyle.

Wherever you are—at home, at school, in the company of friends, traveling—you can find countless small ways to improve your health. Unless you're in a hurry, take the stairs, not the elevator. Think exercise, not TV, during your free time. Find a sport or recreational activity you enjoy. It doesn't matter whether you're destined to become a star athlete; get involved. *Move your body.*

The most obvious and simple form of exercise for families or individuals is walking. Popular now among weight-conscious individuals is the pedometer, a small, inexpensive device you clip to your belt to monitor how many steps you take. Physical therapists say that for most of us, 10,000 steps per day (roughly 5 miles [8 km]) will maintain our current weight level. If your goal is to lose weight, you probably need to walk at least 12,000 to 15,000 steps each day. That sounds like a lot, but you might be surprised how many steps you already take each day, walking back and forth through your school and home. The pedometer is a psychological incentive because it tells the wearer instantly how much progress is being made toward improving fitness.

Rimm describes a healthy lifestyle not in terms of any particular diet or exercise program, but as a "process."[21] It isn't something you pursue until you achieve a particular weight. It's something you should pursue every day for the rest of your life. By regularly keeping watch on your growth, you can avoid the need for drastic measures. Experts cite careful record keeping—noting your weight, exercise routine, and eating patterns—as an excellent aid to weight control.

To help cope with the psychological effects of being overweight, specialists encourage those involved—the overweight individual, parents, friends, and teachers—to emphasize the person's strengths.[22] While working toward a healthy weight, celebrate your progress in schoolwork and find exciting new interests. Never forget that you're a gifted individual who can make great contributions to society.

Running Away from Obesity

Sixteen-year-old Alison began taking charge of her eating and exercise habits three years ago. Until then she was a slightly above-average-weight adolescent who gave little thought to what and when she ate or exercised. She easily could have found herself on the road to a serious weight problem, as did several of her friends. Their lax lifestyles now place them in the at-risk weight category. Happily, when she entered the eighth grade, Alison took a different road. She developed an interest in cross-country running.

She isn't fiercely competitive, but Alison was determined to become a high school varsity runner. She began running with the team almost daily during the winter and spring off-season. At first she was among the slow runners, relegated to the junior varsity. But she was determined. In summer, when training wasn't required, she ran anyway. She steadily built her stamina and speed. Her first great reward came at the end of her ninth-grade year: a varsity letter.

Partly through her coaches' instruction and partly through self-study, she became keenly interested in the types of food and drink a runner should consume or avoid. Alison's daily food consumption doesn't invariably adhere to the MyPyramid plan, but it comes close. She enjoys her mother's home cooking—especially Sunday dinner— and often helps prepare the meal. Alison routinely scrutinizes the ingredients listed in fine print on product packaging. She sometimes indulges in desserts of ice cream, sherbet, or homemade cookies. But she knows exactly what she's eating, and she guards her weight.

Alison rarely drinks soft drinks anymore, preferring cold, bottled water or fruit juice at meals and in between. On weekends, she often goes out to dinner with friends—but she goes mainly to enjoy the company, not to devour food.

If it sounds to you like Alison must be in good shape, you would be right. She feels great, and she's happy and self-confident. Her grades have improved from just above average to an almost straight-A average. Her interest in cross-country running—an easy-to-undertake and rewarding (though somewhat demanding) sport—is obviously an important part of her life.

CHAPTER EIGHT

Dieting and Other Unnatural Remedies

LEARNING TO CONTROL YOUR WEIGHT IS IMPORTANT, ALL HEALTH PROFESSIONALS AGREE—BUT SENSIBLE WEIGHT CONTROL AND DIETING ARE NOT THE SAME THING.

Y ou don't have to search long to find expert advice on how to lose weight. A simple Web query or a quick visit to the health section of a public library will bring to your attention dozens of popular diets—many of them formulated by medical professionals. You'll find Atkins, Jenny Craig, Ornish, Packard, Pritikin, Sears, South Beach, Weight Watchers, and many more. Close by are shelves upon shelves of books on nutrition. They promote anti-aging foods, dairy-free foods, healing foods, mind foods, mood foods, power foods, romance foods, sleep foods, soy foods, spiritual foods, and vegetarian foods. Each diet and nutrition plan promises to improve your health.

It would take years of dedicated research to sort out the distinctions between competing diet programs and to read long-term studies that either support or challenge the various authors. New—often contradictory—findings are headlined regularly in the news media.

It isn't really necessary to compare diet theories and fads. Learning to control your weight is important, all health professionals agree—but sensible weight control and dieting are not the same thing.

DIETS AREN'T NATURAL

The diet "industry"—estimated to be worth anywhere from $6 billion to $50 billion per year[1]—has come under fierce criticism in recent years. "The thinness culture," writes Frances M. Berg in *Underage & Overweight*, "has created a desperation in people at every age, from children to senior citizens, and opportunists are quick to take advantage."[2] Berg contends that of the "hundreds of ways to lose weight fast," none really works.[3]

In their book *The Overweight Child,* Teresa Pittman and Miriam Kaufman concur that "dieting doesn't work, not for adults and not for children." Rather than suggest a diet, they set forth "ideas for changes that can help your entire family become fitter."[4]

Sharron Dalton in *Our Overweight Children* agrees that the solution lies not in dieting but in adjusting behavior. "Overweight kids do not need to 'go on a diet'; they need to eat for their age and be moderately active in order to grow into their weight and develop positive eating habits and active lifestyles."[5] She adds that although successful weight loss programs are shown to improve an individual's self-esteem, this benefit may be only temporary and the long-term results devastating. The risk is a pattern of "yo-yo" weight loss and regaining that in many cases begins in childhood. "Attempts to reshape body size through dieting reinforce feelings of failure and lack of control when they do not produce the expected result. Yet the pursuit of thinness drives the desire to try dieting again—and again."[6]

COMPLICATIONS, COMPLICATIONS

Different types of diets can present different kinds of health complications—even if they all result in weight loss. Among the more controversial popular diet systems in recent years is the one developed by Dr. Robert Atkins. Low in carbohydrates (such as bread) and high in proteins (such as meat), it has been used enthusiastically by millions of weight-conscious individuals. Many have reported that the Atkins diet has not only helped them lose and control their weight but has also reduced their cholesterol levels. However, critics associate low-carb diets with undesirable side effects, including diarrhea, constipation, fatigue, and headaches.[7] They also doubt whether most Atkins dieters—or any other dieters—keep off the weight over time. An estimated 95 percent of all dieters eventually gain back their lost weight.[8]

"Low-fat" diets, meanwhile, have raised concerns among health scientists for several reasons. To begin with, they are rarely advised for preschoolers, since such diets can hurt the child's development.[9] Furthermore, "low-fat" is not necessarily the same as "low-calorie." Examinations have revealed that "low-fat" items on grocery shelves often have the same caloric content as regular products.[10] Food companies began offering many "low-fat" and "no-fat" foods in the early 1990s as a response to Americans' growing concern about obesity and related health problems. Ironically, the obesity problem in America began to accelerate at that point. By 2001, a third of Americans were overweight.[11]

Sugar/fat substitutes, meanwhile, have raised concerns. Saccharin, for example, rang alarms after excessive quantities of it were reported to cause cancer in test animals. Later research has suggested that consumption of small amounts of saccharin probably does not impair human health, but nutritionists do not recommend its regular intake—especially by children.[12] Artificial sweeteners (such as aspartame, neotame, and sucralose, which is also known as Splenda) fool your sweet tooth momentarily, but doctors question whether they're worth the uncertainty. "The majority of these sweeteners are chemical," Dr. Fred Pescatore explains, "and there is no way of knowing the long-term side effects of prolonged consumption."[13]

GOING TO EXTREMES

Overweight individuals often become obsessed with weight loss. They take radical measures that go far beyond the use of sugar substitutes. Negative comments by classmates and relatives often plunge slightly to moderately overweight teenagers into reckless, dangerous dieting. Pescatore, in his book *Feed Your Kids Well*, reports, "By the age of six, nearly 40 percent of American girls have expressed a desire to be thinner. By age nine, nearly 50 percent have dieted once and, by the age of sixteen, 45 percent will have put themselves on some kind of crash diet. Even more disturbing is the fact that 15 percent take diet pills on a regular basis."[14]

For years, millions of Americans have tried diet suppressants and "fat burning" capsules to reduce weight. Most doctors are skeptical of the long-term benefits, and they point to potentially dangerous side effects of certain anti-fat medications.

Summer weight-loss camps for children in recent years have grown in number. Most camps focus on noncompetitive sports and physical activities but also may include arts and crafts, music, and drama. They nurture a sense of belonging among all participants—something many overweight children miss at home and in school. Predictably, food is controlled and proportioned. Camps are intended to result not just in on-site weight loss but long-term health habits that will give the child lifelong control over weight problems. While numerous success stories have been chronicled, many frustrated participants have equated them with military boot camps and have realized no meaningful benefits. Health observers agree that obesity camps are unlikely to solve your problem unless you can, in fact, follow up by changing your long-term eating and exercise habits.[15]

Some severely obese individuals have resorted to radical solutions. These measures are controversial, even among adults. One that became popular in America during the 1980s is suction lipectomy, or "liposuction." A form of cosmetic surgery, it literally uses a suction tube to remove fat through tiny skin incisions. Liposuction is typically used in efforts to reshape specific areas of the body, such as the thighs.

Another surgical procedure requested by some obese individuals is the gastric bypass. The stomach is made smaller by closing off a large section of it with surgical staples. The intestinal system then is reconnected to the small upper section. Result: Since only a fraction of the stomach is used for digestion, the patient feels full after consuming only a fraction as much food as before.

Only in unusual circumstances are such unnatural remedies recommended, even for adults. Each presents medical risks—risks that need not concern you if, while you're young, you learn to control your weight with discipline and informed health habits.

COMMON SENSE—THE BEST MEDICINE

Almost all medical experts agree that obesity is a widespread health hazard. There is less agreement on how to confront it. So far, many of the attempts to reverse and control obesity have presented health risks of their own. A study of more than five thousand overweight men, for example, concluded that those who lost the most weight tended to die younger than those who lost none.[16] Separate studies have indicated that radical low-calorie diets may increase the risk of heart ailments.[17] And ironically, dieting in many cases has resulted, over time, in weight gain.[18] In their book *The Overweight Child*, Teresa Pitman and Miriam Kaufman write that "the cycle of weight loss, followed by regaining weight, losing it again and gaining it back again is much more dangerous to health than maintaining a high but steady weight."[19]

Pitman and Kaufman emphatically discourage diets for young people.[20]

TEN GREAT QUESTIONS TO ASK WHEN SEEKING HELP

Your first step in coping with a problem of excessive weight should be to get the facts. Here are some practical questions you might pose to your doctor or dietician.

1. I have friends who eat french fries all the time, and they aren't fat. What's different about me?
2. Both my mom and dad are average size—and my sister is even skinny. We eat pretty much the same things. Why am I overweight and they're not?
3. Which is more important for weight control: careful eating habits or increased exercise?
4. If I start today, how long will it take me to achieve a healthy weight?
5. Why can't I use fat-burning pills and appetite suppressants?
6. Is there anything wrong with skipping meals or other forms of fasting?
7. What makes dining out more fattening than eating at home with the family?
8. Can I lose weight by eating mostly cold foods rather than hot meals?
9. If I lose too much weight too fast, will I become anorexic?
10. Will I always have to struggle to control my appetite and my weight? Is there no permanent solution?

Many dieticians and nutritionists will work with you individually to help you find a healthy approach to eating and exercising.

CHAPTER NINE

Signs of Progress

MORE THAN ANYTHING ELSE, AMERICANS SIMPLY NEED TO RETURN TO EATING AND EXERCISE HABITS SIMILAR TO THOSE PRACTICED BY OLDER GENERATIONS.

N utritionists, doctors, and public health officials agree that sensible eating habits and regular exercise are important to good health. That's true for you, regardless of your height, frame, heredity, or home situation. If you're in good physical condition, you need to be mindful of your eating and activity habits so you'll stay that way. If you're overweight, you can change—and it may not be as difficult as you think.

Preschool children naturally have little control in making decisions that result in a healthy lifestyle. For the most part, parents determine what they will eat—or, at least, what their food and drink choices will be—and what kinds of exercise they will get. As you grew older, you began making many of those decisions yourself. Meanwhile, your school and community increasingly began to influence your lifestyle. Health and social science professionals believe that in addition to individual efforts, school and community leaders can go far to curb the obesity epidemic.

CONFRONTING THE PROBLEM

Encouraging steps are being taken, especially in schools. For example, some school cafeterias have developed creative menus that offer truly appetizing vegetable and fruit selections.[1] Many school systems have removed soft drink and snack machines from school grounds. Teachers and parents are becoming aware that the sale of doughnuts, candy, and cookies in fund-raising drives sends conflicting signals to youngsters who are taking an interest in wise nutrition.[2]

Progress in schools has been slow because it can be costly. When a California school district voted to end snack sales in 2003, its annual revenue was reduced by more than half a million dollars.[3] But with rising public alarm over the obesity crisis, school administrators realize that contributing to better health among students is worth the price, in the long run.

Teachers and parents can play a significant role in helping overweight children. If nothing more, they can encourage them in their special gifts, strengths, and accomplishments, thus boosting their self-confidence. This psychological support can foster an overall attitude change. In her studies, Dr. Sylvia Rimm found that this is already being demonstrated. "When teachers were able to focus on students' strengths and develop an alliance, they enabled students to do something about their problems."[4]

On a different front, the food industry has begun taking measures to counter obesity—although not as aggressively as some critics would like. Food companies have adjusted the ingredients in certain products to make them healthier, and they've contributed funds to health education programs.[5] Some have begun to provide nutritional labels that are easier to understand. As you know, food marketers list the ingredients of each product on the packaging. The numbers may mean nothing to you, though, unless you've studied food science.

Overall, efforts to correct dangerous weight trends are producing only slight success. Americans of all ages, by most accounts, still tend to overeat and under-exercise—and to prefer foods high in sugar and calories. But a variety of programs have shown promise in promoting a healthier America.

PROMISING PROGRAMS

You may want to investigate some of the following programs that could contribute to your well-being.

- Eat Well and *Keep Moving*, a program developed by the Harvard School of Public Health (whose main campus is located in Boston, Massachusetts), teaches children about healthy nutrition and fitness practices. It has produced exciting results in test projects, beginning in 1997. After participating in the program, children in fourteen Baltimore, Maryland, schools were found to be eating more fruits and vegetables and fewer fats, improving their understanding of fitness and nutrition, and watching less television.
- KidsWalk-to-School is part of the Nutrition and Physical Activity Program of the national Centers for Disease Control and Prevention. Its objective is to bring together individuals and organizations in different communities to create safe walking and biking routes to and from school. Adult volunteers make this happen by accompanying groups of student bikers and pedestrians.

- SHAPEDOWN is a children's weight-loss program developed by faculty members of the School of Medicine at the University of California, San Francisco. A survey of participants reported "significantly decreased relative weight and significantly improved weight-related behavior," including self-esteem, depression tendencies, and health knowledge.
- The America on the Move Foundation (AOM) inspires citizens to engage in fun ways to achieve and maintain a healthy weight. Its objective is to get the average American to make two simple lifestyle changes every day: eat 100 fewer calories (roughly equivalent to a single pat of butter) and walk 2,000 additional steps (approximately 1 extra mile [1.6 km]). AOM supports a network of state affiliates.

On the Internet, in a matter of minutes you can gather useful resources to help you begin dealing with obesity. Numerous federal and state government, medical, and academic institutions offer valuable weight-related information, programs, research statistics, and consumer advice. Much of it is available online at no cost. Meanwhile, books and other printed and video material on the topic can be found at your school or local public library.

Be aware, however, that much "junk health" misinformation is also distributed online and in print. The most reliable Internet sites are those developed by government agencies (.gov) and educational institutions (.edu), along with some of the related sites to which they link.

A VITAL CHALLENGE

In 2000, the U.S. Department of Health and Human Services formulated a "Healthy People 2010" plan. It's intended to reduce the percentage of overweight Americans to 5 percent by the year 2010. Observers doubt that will be accomplished, based on statistical trends in the opening years of the new century.[6] It's crucial that we try, however. Controlling the obesity problem not only is something we *can* do; it's something we *must* do. Rimm warns in her book, "Unless the problem is addressed and efforts are made on many fronts, the next generation is destined to see a precipitous rise in the chronic disease burden from diabetes, heart disease, cancer, and numerous other serious health consequences."[7]

Health professionals don't expect quick changes. Our national weight problems result from unwise changes in our eating and exercise patterns over half a century. Reversing the trend will likewise be gradual.

Americans don't need an elaborate new health strategy, professionals believe. More than anything else, Americans simply need to return to eating and exercise habits similar to those practiced by older generations.[8] If you're concerned about weight at this point in your life, be assured the problem can be remedied. Common sense and a bit of discipline are the best "medicines"—and they're free.

aerobic Affecting breathing and circulation in the body.

à la carte Sold separately. Basing your school lunchroom fare on à la carte menu items such as french fries and desserts can contribute to weight gain.

calorie A measure of heat. Specific foods provide differing numbers of caloric units, or energy-producing values, to the human body. Various forms of exercise "burn" differing amounts of calories.

carbohydrate A heat-producing body nutrient. Some carb types are sugars, others are starches or fibers.

cardiovascular Having to do with the heart, veins, and vessels.

cholesterol A soft substance in the bloodstream necessary to produce certain vitamins, acids, and other essentials. Excessive cholesterol, caused by overcon-sumption of certain fatty foods, can hinder circulation and dam-age vital organs.

glucose A form of sugar gener-ally derived from cornstarch.

gluttony The tendency to overeat.

hypertension Abnormally high blood pressure.

insulin A hormone produced by the body to regulate sugar levels in the bloodstream.

mono fat A type of unsaturated fat found in oils such as olive oil and peanut oil.

nutrition The process of nourishing the body with essential combinations of food types.

osteoarthritis A disease brought about by constant stress on the human joints.

pancreas A human gland that secretes insulin and other hormones into the bloodstream.

poly fat A type of unsaturated fat found in such plants as corn, sunflower, and soybean oils.

respiratory Related to the lungs and the system that circulates oxygen through the body.

saturated fat A type of fat typically obtained from meat and dairy products; overconsumption of this fat can result in damage to the heart and circulatory system.

serotonin A bodily chemical that affects the performance of the brain, cardiovascular system, and other functions. Serotonin levels can be altered by stress and can affect the appetite.

sleep apnea Momentary interruptions to breathing while you're asleep.

trans fat A type of fat containing unsaturated fatty acids, which have been linked to high cholesterol levels.

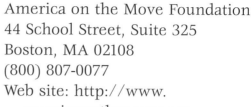

America on the Move Foundation
44 School Street, Suite 325
Boston, MA 02108
(800) 807-0077
Web site: http://www.
americaonthemove.org

A national initiative to support healthy eating and active living habits among individuals and communities.

Canada's Physical Activity Guides
   for Children and Youth
Public Health Agency of Canada
Physical Activity Unit
Tunney's Pasture, Address Locator:
   1907C1
Ottawa, ON K1A 1B4
(613) 941-3109
Web site: http://www.phac-aspc.gc.
   ca/pau-uap/paguide/child_
   youth.index.html

Links to related resources, guides, and other information available on the Internet.

Centers for Disease Control and
   Prevention (CDC)
U.S. Department of Health and
   Human Services
1600 Clifton Road
Atlanta, GA 30333
(404) 639-3534 or (800) 311-3435
Web site: http://www.cdc.gov

The CDC offers a number of Web pages pertaining to obesity and related health concerns.

childobesity.com
1323 San Anselmo Avenue
San Anselmo, CA 94960
(415) 453-8886
Web site: http://www.childobesity.com

This site provides links to a variety of child obesity resources, including the SHAPEDOWN obesity intervention program (www.shapedown.com).

Eat Well and *Keep Moving*
Harvard School of Public Health
Department of Nutrition
665 Huntington Avenue, 2-253a
Boston, MA 02115
(617) 432-1086
Web site: http://www.hsph.harvard.edu/
    nutritionsource/EWKM.html

A children's educational program designed to equip children with the information they need to choose healthy diets and physical activities.

WEB SITES

Due to the changing nature of Internet links, Rosen Publishing has developed an online list of Web sites related to the subject of this book. This site is updated regularly. Please use this link to access the list:

http://www.rosenlinks.com/ccw/obes

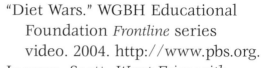

"Diet Wars." WGBH Educational
Foundation *Frontline* series
video. 2004. http://www.pbs.org.
Ingram, Scott. *Want Fries with
That?: Obesity and the Supersizing
of America* (Watts Library). New
York, NY: Franklin Watts, 2005.
Kay, Kathlyn. *Am I Fat?: The
Obesity Issue for Teens* (Issues in
Focus Today). Berkeley Heights,
NJ: Enslow Publishers, 2006.
Kramer, Gerri Freid, and Mark J.
Kittleson, ed. *The Truth About
Eating Disorders*. New York, NY:
Facts on File, 2004.
Lawton, Sandra A. *Eating Disorders
Information for Teens: Health
Tips About Anorexia, Bulimia,
Binge Eating, and Other Eating
Disorders* (Teen Health Series).
Detroit, MI: Omnigraphics, 2005.
Owens, Peter. *Teens Health and
Obesity* (The Gallup Youth
Survey: Major Issues and
Trends). Broomall, PA: Mason
Crest Publishers, 2005.
Schlosser, Eric. *Chew on This:
Everything You Don't Want to
Know About Fast Food*. Boston,
MA: Houghton Mifflin, 2006.

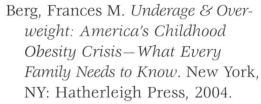

Berg, Frances M. *Underage & Overweight: America's Childhood Obesity Crisis—What Every Family Needs to Know*. New York, NY: Hatherleigh Press, 2004.

Caldwell, Wilma, and Chad T. Kimball, eds. *Obesity Sourcebook*, 1st ed. Detroit, MI: Omnigraphics, 2001.

Critser, Greg. *Fat Land: How Americans Became the Fattest People in the World*. Boston, MA: Houghton Mifflin Company, 2003.

Dalton, Sharron. *Our Overweight Children: What Parents, Schools, and Communities Can Do to Control the Fatness Epidemic*. Berkeley, CA: University of California Press, 2004.

Dreyfuss, Ira. "Fat Camps Can Cause Yo-Yo Weights." Associated Press, August 12, 2003. Retrieved March 9, 2006 (http://www. cbsnews.com/ stories/2003/08/12/health/ main567923.shtml).

Groch, Judith. "Atkins Dieter Develops Life-Threatening Complications." *MedPage Today*, March 17, 2006. Retrieved April 3, 2006 (http:// www. medpagetoday.com/tbid = 2878).

Hirsch, J.M. "Food Companies a Target for Obesity Problem." Associated Press, *Spartanburg Herald-Journal*, March 19, 2006.

"Limiting Sugary Drinks Slows Teens' Weight Gain." Consumeraffairs.com, March 6, 2006. Retrieved April 5, 2006 (http://www.consumeraffairs.com/news04/2006/03/teens_sugary_drinks.html).

"McDonalds Finds More Trans Fat in Its Fries." Consumeraffairs.com, February 8, 2006. Retrieved April 4, 2006 (http://www.consumeraffairs.com/news04/2006/02/mcdonalds_fries.html).

Mitchell, Stacy Ann, and Teri D. Mitchell. *Livin' Large: African American Sisters Confront Obesity*. Roscoe, IL: Hilton Publishing Company, 2004.

Mitchell, Susan, and Catherine Christie. *I'd Kill for a Cookie: A Simple Six-Week Plan to Conquer Stress Eating*. New York, NY: Dutton/Penguin, 1997.

Pescatore, Fred. *Feed Your Kids Well: How to Help Your Child Lose Weight and Get Healthy*. Hoboken, NJ: John Wiley & Sons, Inc., 1998.

Pitman, Teresa, and Miriam Kaufman. *The Overweight Child: Promoting Fitness and Self-Esteem*. Buffalo, NY: Firefly Books Ltd., 2000.

Pool, Robert. *Fat: Fighting the Obesity Epidemic*. New York, NY: Oxford University Press, Inc., 2001.

Rimm, Dr. Sylvia. *Rescuing the Emotional Lives of Overweight Children*. Emmaeus, PA: Rodale, 2004.

Roberts, Susan B., and Melvin B. Heyman. *Feeding Your Child for Lifelong Health: Birth Through Age Six*. New York, NY: Bantam Books, 1999.

Shanley, Ellen, and Colleen Thompson. *Fueling the Teen Machine*. Palo Alto, CA: Bull Publishing Company, 2001.

Tamborlane, William V., ed. *The Yale Guide to Children's Nutrition*. New Haven, CT: Yale University Press, 1997.

Tanner, Lindsey. "Car Seats Straining to Hold Heavier Kids." Associated Press, *Spartanburg Herald-Journal*, April 3, 2006.

Tartamella, Lisa, et al. *Generation Extra Large: Rescuing Our Children from the Epidemic of Obesity*. New York, NY: Basic Books, 2004.

Torgan, Carol. "Childhood Obesity on the Rise." *Word on Health* (National Institutes of Health), June 2002. Retrieved March 8, 2006 (http://www.nih.gov/news/WordonHealth/june2002/childhoodobesity.htm).

"Virus Could Mean Obesity Is Contagious." *Medical Study News*, January 30, 2006. Retrieved April 3, 2006 (http://www.news-medical.net/?id=15686).

"Youth Obesity Rising Faster Among Poor, Study Says." Associated Press, May 24, 2006. Retrieved May 30, 2006 (http://www.boston.com/news/nation/articles/2006/05/24/youth_obesity_rising_faster_among_poor_study_says).

Chapter 1

1. National Center for Health Statistics (www.cdc.gov/nchs).
2. Sharron Dalton, *Our Overweight Children: What Parents, Schools, and Communities Can Do to Control the Fatness Epidemic* (Berkeley, CA: University of California Press, 2004), pp. 2, 29.
3. Ibid., p. 31.
4. Stacy Ann Mitchell and Teri D. Mitchell, *Livin' Large: African American Sisters Confront Obesity* (Roscoe, IL: Hilton Publishing Company, 2004), p. 3.
5. Frances M. Berg, *Underage & Overweight: America's Childhood Obesity Crisis—What Every Family Needs to Know* (New York, NY: Hatherleigh Press, 2004), p. 4.
6. Dalton, p. 29.
7. Lindsey Tanner, "Car Seats Straining to Hold Heavier Kids," Associated Press, April 3, 2006 (*Spartanburg Herald-Journal*).
8. National Center for Health Statistics (http://www.cdc.gov/nchs).
9. "Diet Wars," WGBH Educational Foundation *Frontline* series video (http://www.pbs.org), 2004.
10. Sylvia Rimm, *Rescuing the Emotional Lives of Overweight Children* (Emmaeus, PA: Rodale, 2004), p. 20.

11. Greg Critser, *Fat Land: How Americans Became the Fattest People in the World* (Boston, MA: Houghton Mifflin Company, 2003), p. 158.
12. Dalton, p. 86.
13. J. M. Hirsch, "Food Companies a Target for Obesity Problem," Associated Press, March 19, 2006 (*Spartanburg Herald-Journal*).
14. Ibid.
15. Berg, p. 59.
16. Ibid., p. 59.
17. Dalton, p. 107.
18. Ibid., p. 82.
19. Ibid., p. 2.
20. Rimm, foreword.
21. Fred Pescatore, *Feed Your Kids Well: How to Help Your Child Lose Weight and Get Healthy* (Hoboken, NJ: John Wiley & Sons, Inc., 1998), p. 22.

Chapter 2

1. Dan McMillan, *Obesity* (New York, NY: Franklin Watts, 1994), pp. 13–14.
2. Teresa Pitman and Miriam Kaufman, *The Overweight Child: Promoting Fitness and Self-Esteem* (Buffalo, NY: Firefly Books Ltd., 2000), p. 20.
3. Barbara Moe, *Understanding Negative Body Image* (New York, NY: Rosen Publishing, 1999), p. 14.
4. Sharron Dalton, *Our Overweight Children: What Parents, Schools, and Communities Can Do to Control the Fatness Epidemic* (Berkeley, CA: University of California Press, 2004), p. 26.
5. Frances M. Berg, *Underage & Overweight: America's Childhood Obesity Crisis—What Every Family Needs to Know* (New York, NY: Hatherleigh Press, 2004), p. 4.
6. Dalton, p. 23.

7. Ibid.
8. Robert Pool, *Fat: Fighting the Obesity Epidemic* (New York, NY: Oxford University Press, Inc., 2001), p. 25.
9. William V. Tamborlane, ed., *The Yale Guide to Children's Nutrition* (New Haven, CT: Yale University Press, 1997), p. 94.

Chapter 3
1. "Limiting Sugary Drinks Slows Teens' Weight Gain," Consumeraffairs.com, March 6, 2006. Retrieved April 5, 2006 (http://www.consumeraffairs.com/news04/2006/03/teens_sugary_drinks.html).
2. Frances M. Berg, *Underage & Overweight: America's Childhood Obesity Crisis—What Every Family Needs to Know* (New York, NY: Hatherleigh Press, 2004), p. 76.
3. Stacy Ann Mitchell and Teri D. Mitchell, *Livin' Large: African American Sisters Confront Obesity* (Roscoe, IL: Hilton Publishing Company, 2004), p. 24.
4. Sharron Dalton, *Our Overweight Children: What Parents, Schools, and Communities Can Do to Control the Fatness Epidemic* (Berkeley, CA: University of California Press, 2004), p. 113.
5. J. M. Hirsch, "Food Companies a Target for Obesity Problem," Associated Press, March 19, 2006 (*Spartanburg Herald-Journal*).
6. Sylvia Rimm, *Rescuing the Emotional Lives of Overweight Children* (Emmaeus, PA: Rodale, 2004), p. 25.
7. Susan B. Roberts and Melvin B. Heyman, *Feeding Your Child for Lifelong Health: Birth Through Age Six* (New York, NY: Bantam Books, 1999), p. 219.
8. Hirsch.
9. Dalton, p. 93.
10. Lisa Tartamella, et al., *Generation Extra Large: Rescuing Our Children from the Epidemic of Obesity* (New York, NY: Basic Books, 2004), p. 78.

11. Ibid., pp. 79–80.
12. Ibid., p. 80.
13. Dalton, pp. 98–104.
14. Hirsch.
15. Dalton, p. 82.
16. William V. Tamborlane, ed. *The Yale Guide to Children's Nutrition* (New Haven, CT: Yale University Press, 1997), p. 283.
17. Rimm, p. 118.
18. Berg, p. 58.
19. Rimm, p. 23.
20. Dalton, p. 86.
21. Ibid., p. 86.
22. Rimm, p. 23.
23. Ibid., p. 109.
24. Dalton, p. 87.

Chapter 4

1. Teresa Pitman and Miriam Kaufman, *The Overweight Child: Promoting Fitness and Self-Esteem* (Buffalo, NY: Firefly Books Ltd., 2000), p. 33.
2. Susan B. Roberts and Melvin B. Heyman, *Feeding Your Child for Lifelong Health: Birth Through Age Six* (New York, NY: Bantam Books, 1999), p. 207.
3. Sharron Dalton, *Our Overweight Children: What Parents, Schools, and Communities Can Do to Control the Fatness Epidemic* (Berkeley, CA: University of California Press, 2004), p. 80.
4. Ibid., p. 54.
5. Ibid., p. 84.
6. Ibid., p. 83.
7. Sylvia Rimm, *Rescuing the Emotional Lives of Overweight Children* (Emmaeus, PA: Rodale, 2004), pp. 174–175.
8. Dalton, p. 77.
9. Ibid., p. 61.

10. Frances M. Berg, *Underage & Overweight: America's Childhood Obesity Crisis—What Every Family Needs to Know* (New York, NY: Hatherleigh Press, 2004), p. 5.
11. Dalton, p. 31.
12. Ibid., p. 33.
13. Ibid., pp. 54–55.
14. "Youth Obesity Rising Faster Among Poor, Study Says," Associated Press, May 24, 2006. Retrieved May 30, 2006 (http://www.boston.com/news/nation/articles/2006/05/24/youth_obesity_rising_faster_among_poor_study_says).
15. Dalton, p. 56.
16. Ibid., p. 22.
17. Ibid., p. 24.
18. Ibid., pp. 33–34.
19. Ibid., p. 34.
20. Ibid., p. 37.
21. Robert Pool, *Fat: Fighting the Obesity Epidemic* (New York, NY: Oxford University Press, Inc., 2001), p. 154.
22. Rimm, p. 16.
23. Teresa Pitman and Miriam Kaufman, *The Overweight Child: Promoting Fitness and Self-Esteem* (Buffalo, NY: Firefly Books Ltd., 2000), p. 19.
24. Rimm, p. 26.
25. Fred Pescatore, *Feed Your Kids Well: How to Help Your Child Lose Weight and Get Healthy* (Hoboken, NJ: John Wiley & Sons, Inc., 1998), p. 14.
26. Pitman, p. 34.
27. Ibid., p. 31.
28. Wilma Caldwell and Chad T. Kimball, eds., *Obesity Sourcebook*, 1st ed. (Detroit, MI: Omnigraphics, 2001), p. 236.
29. Dalton, pp. 46–47.
30. Ibid., p. 47.

31. Rimm, p. 22.
32. Ibid., p. 124.
33. Ibid., p. 34.
34. "Virus Could Mean Obesity Is Contagious," *Medical Study News*, January 30, 2006. Retrieved April 3, 2006 (http://www.news-medical.net/?id=15686).
35. Pitman, p. 28.

Chapter 5

1. Sharron Dalton, *Our Overweight Children: What Parents, Schools, and Communities Can Do to Control the Fatness Epidemic* (Berkeley, CA: University of California Press, 2004), p. 32.
2. Ibid., p. 13.
3. Sylvia Rimm, *Rescuing the Emotional Lives of Overweight Children* (Emmaeus, PA: Rodale, 2004), p. 19.
4. Dalton, p. 15.
5. Ibid., p. 17.
6. Ibid., p. 20.
7. Ibid., p. 21.
8. Teresa Pitman and Miriam Kaufman, *The Overweight Child: Promoting Fitness and Self-Esteem* (Buffalo, NY: Firefly Books Ltd., 2000), p. 18.
9. Ibid., p. 19.
10. J. M. Hirsch, "Food Companies a Target for Obesity Problem," Associated Press, March 19, 2006 (*Spartanburg Herald-Journal*).
11. Fred Pescatore, *Feed Your Kids Well: How to Help Your Child Lose Weight and Get Healthy* (Hoboken, NJ: John Wiley & Sons, Inc., 1998), p. 54.
12. Ibid., p. 58.
13. Dalton, p. 158.
14. Ibid., p. 159.
15. "McDonalds Finds More Trans Fat in Its Fries," Consumeraffairs.com, February 8, 2006. Retrieved

April 4, 2006 (http://www.consumeraffairs.com/
news04/2006/02/mcdonalds_fries.html).
16. Dalton, p. 110.
17. Rimm, p. 18.
18. Dalton, pp. 161–164.
19. Frances M. Berg, *Underage & Overweight:
America's Childhood Obesity Crisis—What Every
Family Needs to Know* (New York, NY: Hatherleigh
Press, 2004), p. 313.
20. Dalton, p. 81.
21. Ibid.
22. Ellen Shanley and Colleen Thompson, *Fueling the
Teen Machine* (Palo Alto, CA: Bull Publishing
Company, 2001), pp. 131–132.
23. Dalton, p. 97.
24. Berg, p. 118.
25. Stacy Ann Mitchell and Teri D. Mitchell, *Livin' Large:
African American Sisters Confront Obesity* (Roscoe,
IL: Hilton Publishing Company, 2004), p. 37.
26. Dalton, p. 26.

Chapter 6

1. Teresa Pitman and Miriam Kaufman, *The Overweight Child: Promoting Fitness and Self-Esteem*
(Buffalo, NY: Firefly Books Ltd., 2000), p. 19.
2. Sharron Dalton, *Our Overweight Children: What
Parents, Schools, and Communities Can Do to Control
the Fatness Epidemic* (Berkeley, CA: University of
California Press, 2004), p. 5.
3. Ibid., p. 38.
4. "Diet Wars," WGBH Educational Foundation
Frontline series video (http://www.pbs.org), 2004.
5. Dalton, p. 39.
6. Ibid., p. 37.

7. Ibid., p. 38.
8. Ibid., pp. 36, 39.
9. Ibid., p. 36.
10. Dan McMillan, *Obesity* (New York, NY: Franklin Watts, 1994), p. 49.
11. Dalton, p. 36.
12. Ibid.
13. Pitman, p. 12.
14. Sylvia Rimm, *Rescuing the Emotional Lives of Overweight Children* (Emmaeus, PA: Rodale, 2004), foreword.
15. Dalton, p. 40.
16. Rimm, p. 35.
17. Susan B. Roberts and Melvin B. Heyman, *Feeding Your Child for Lifelong Health: Birth Through Age Six* (New York, NY: Bantam Books, 1999), p. 223.
18. Rimm, p. 39.
19. Ibid., p. 8.
20. Ibid., p. 35.
21. Ibid., p. 51.
22. Ibid., p. 78.
23. Ibid., p. 165.
24. Ibid., p. 86.
25. Dalton, p. 201.
26. Ibid., p. 4.
27. Ibid., p. 35.

Chapter 7

1. Sharron Dalton, *Our Overweight Children: What Parents, Schools, and Communities Can Do to Control the Fatness Epidemic* (Berkeley, CA: University of California Press, 2004), p. 7.
2. Susan B. Roberts and Melvin B. Heyman, *Feeding Your Child for Lifelong Health: Birth*

Through Age Six (New York, NY: Bantam Books, 1999), p. 12.

3. Ibid., p. 113.
4. Dalton, pp. 121–124.
5. Fred Pescatore, *Feed Your Kids Well: How to Help Your Child Lose Weight and Get Healthy* (Hoboken, NJ: John Wiley & Sons, Inc., 1998), p. 210.
6. Ellen Shanley and Colleen Thompson, *Fueling the Teen Machine* (Palo Alto, CA: Bull Publishing Company, 2001), p. 6.
7. Ibid., p. 7.
8. Sylvia Rimm, *Rescuing the Emotional Lives of Overweight Children* (Emmaeus, PA: Rodale, 2004), p. 133.
9. Roberts, p. 125.
10. Rimm, p. 108.
11. Ibid., p. 187.
12. Pescatore, p. 229.
13. Dalton, p. 165.
14. Ibid., p. 86.
15. Frances M. Berg, *Underage & Overweight: America's Childhood Obesity Crisis—What Every Family Needs to Know* (New York, NY: Hatherleigh Press, 2004), p. 313.
16. Rimm, pp. 120–121.
17. Ibid., p. 121.
18. Ibid., p. 123.
19. Ibid.
20. Ibid., p. 128.
21. Ibid., p. 202.
22. Ibid., p. 209.

Chapter 8

1. Sharron Dalton, *Our Overweight Children: What Parents, Schools, and Communities Can Do to Control*

the Fatness Epidemic (Berkeley, CA: University of California Press, 2004), p. 45.

2. Frances M. Berg, *Underage & Overweight: America's Childhood Obesity Crisis—What Every Family Needs to Know* (New York, NY: Hatherleigh Press, 2004), p. 159.
3. Ibid., p. 158.
4. Teresa Pitman and Miriam Kaufman, *The Overweight Child: Promoting Fitness and Self-Esteem* (Buffalo, NY: Firefly Books Ltd., 2000), p. 15.
5. Dalton, p. 175.
6. Ibid., p. 41.
7. Judith Groch, "Atkins Dieter Develops Life-Threatening Complications," *MedPage Today*, March 17, 2006. Retrieved April 3, 2006 (http://www.medpagetoday.com/tbid=2878).
8. Pitman, p. 18.
9. Susan B. Roberts and Melvin B. Heyman, *Feeding Your Child for Lifelong Health: Birth Through Age Six* (New York, NY: Bantam Books, 1999), p. 128.
10. Ibid.
11. "Diet Wars," WGBH Educational Foundation *Frontline* series video (http://www.pbs.org), 2004.
12. Roberts, p. 129.
13. Fred Pescatore, *Feed Your Kids Well: How to Help Your Child Lose Weight and Get Healthy* (Hoboken, NJ: John Wiley & Sons, Inc., 1998), p. 47.
14. Ibid., pp. 15–16.
15. Ira Dreyfuss, "Fat Camps Can Cause Yo-Yo Weights," Associated Press, August 12, 2003. Retrieved March 9, 2006 (http://www.cbsnews.com/stories/2003/08/12/health/main567923.shtml).
16. Pitman, p. 18.
17. Ibid.

18. Ibid., p. 19.
19. Ibid., pp. 13, 18.
20. Ibid., p. 28.

Chapter 9

1. Sharron Dalton, *Our Overweight Children: What Parents, Schools, and Communities Can Do to Control the Fatness Epidemic* (Berkeley, CA: University of California Press, 2004), p. 104.
2. Ibid., p. 99.
3. Ibid., p. 100.
4. Sylvia Rimm, *Rescuing the Emotional Lives of Overweight Children* (Emmaeus, PA: Rodale, 2004), p. 96.
5. J. M. Hirsch, "Food Companies a Target for Obesity Problem," Associated Press, March 19, 2006 (*Spartanburg Herald-Journal*).
6. Frances M. Berg, *Underage & Overweight: America's Childhood Obesity Crisis—What Every Family Needs to Know* (New York, NY: Hatherleigh Press, 2004), p. 4.
7. Rimm, p. 33.
8. Dalton, p. 6.

INDEX

About the Author

Daniel E. Harmon is a veteran magazine and newspaper editor and a writer whose articles have appeared in many national and regional periodicals. His juvenile educational books include psychological studies of Alzheimer's disease, anorexia nervosa, manic depression, and schizophrenia, as well as books on government agencies including the Food and Drug Administration and the Environmental Protection Agency. He lives in Spartanburg, South Carolina.